A GUIDE TO ALTERNATIVE MEDICINE

Other Books by Donald Law:

CONCISE HERBAL ENCYCLOPEDIA
HERB-GROWING FOR HEALTH
HERBAL TEAS FOR HEALTH AND PLEASURE
HOW TO DEFEAT RHEUMATISM AND ARTHRITIS
HERBS FOR HEALTH AND HEALING
HOW TO KEEP YOUR HAIR ON
HERBS FOR COOKING AND HEALING
TEXTBOOK OF BOTANIC MEDICINE (8 VOLUMES)
DEGREE COURSE IN PHILOSOPHY
BEGINNER'S GUIDE TO SAILING
BEGINNER'S GUIDE TO SWIMMING AND WATER SPORTS
THE YOUNG PERSON'S NATURE GUIDE
ASTROLOGY, PALMISTRY AND DREAMS
HANDBUCH DER HEILKRÄUTER
LUONNONVARAISTA TERVEYSTEETÄ

A Guide
to
Alternative
Medicine

DONALD LAW
Ph.D., D.B.M., Psy.D.

DOLPHIN BOOKS
DOUBLEDAY & COMPANY, INC.
GARDEN CITY, NEW YORK
1976

Dolphin edition: 1976
Originally published in Great Britain
by Turnstone Books
and in the United States
by Hippocrene Books, Inc., 1975.

ISBN: 0-385-11583-0

Dedicated to my friends Arto Vähällä the concert pianist and Rita Honkala the singer.

Thank you for your beautiful music!

Mi oli miehiä lähellä, ne kaikki lakit käessä; mi oli akkoja lähellä, ne kaikki käsi posella. Tyttäret vesissä silmin, pojat maassa polvillansa, kanteloista kuuntelivat, iloa imehtelivät. Sanoivat samalla suulla, yhen kielen kerkesivät: Ei ole tutoa ennen kuultu noin suloista soitantoa, sinä ilmoisna ikänä, kuuna kullan valkeana!

Runo 54. Kalevala

Acknowledgment

I wish to place on record my sincere thanks to Alick Bartholomew for his kind help and patience in the preparation of this book.

Donald Law
Linnunlaulula, 1974

CONTENTS

PART I Why Alternative Medicine?

PART II The Guide to Alternative Medicine

PART III **Going Further**

LIST OF ILLUSTRATIONS

Part one

WHY
ALTERNATIVE MEDICINE?

1.

THE ART
OF HEALING THE SICK

Archaeological research indicates that the origin of the Garden of Eden legend was most likely Dhahran, near Bahrein. Apart from legendary perfection, sickness and disease have been present among the human species more or less from the dawn of recorded history. Equally present in the human spirit has been a desire to heal, to replace foul with fair, corruption with perfection, and sickness with restored health.

What is today known as medicine is the accretion of knowledge about healing over many centuries, even millennia, colored by the prevailing political and economic influences of the times. For instance, bathing in the spring sacred to Diana as a means of healing ceased to be therapeutic under the Edicts of Constantine (A.D. 312), which declared Christianity the sole religion of the Roman Empire.

It is interesting to observe the forms which did survive, with or without official approval, and to search for the guiding principles which lead to the acceptance or rejection of theories, for many branches of healing rest upon little but hypothesis and observation.

The basic idea which links most of us interested in the subject is that of healing. We must accustom ourselves to the fact that there is much which seems impossible to us, just as five centuries ago to talk of laser beams or live television transmissions bounced off the surface of the moon would have assuredly led one to the stake, comforted by the tears and prayers of Torquemada.

In examining the different forms of healing discussed here the reader is cautioned against feeling too much emotion in favor of or against any one method. The objects of this book are twofold: firstly, to place on record such forms of healing as have been known to produce results but which are not generally practiced by the established medical schools of the Western world (herbalism and acupuncture are widely practiced in China by state-qualified doctors); secondly, to encourage independent research and experimentation by all medical men who would rather concentrate on the need to know and to heal, than merely to continue unquestioningly in traditional paths.

Where there is no criticism there will be no progress, and the outlook of a civilization devoid of progress is most uninviting. 'A blind soul is a tyrant'[1], Camus tells us in *Caligula*. History, particularly that of our own century, has shown that intellectual myopia and tyranny often go hand in hand, or that where one goes the other frequently follows. We should study every method of healing as a matter of principle.

This book is to help practicing medical men as much as the layman in search of health. We must be generous toward the intention of the established medical schools' practitioners. Their course of studies is extremely arduous; it certainly leaves most of them no time to consider whether what they are taught is wholly or universally efficacious. While most doctors themselves would reject the soap-opera image of saints in surgical gloves such as depicted by the excellent television series, amusing novels and films, we also cannot accept that they are just sales agents for the pharmaceutical companies' products, which some fringe groups imply. Most doctors barely get time to study the enormous quantity of advertising literature which pharmaceutical houses send to them, quite apart from conducting research into other forms of healing.

Here then are some details of healing arts which have survived. Leonardo da Vinci said: 'Truth is the only daughter of Time.' Many people go to the alternative healing arts for health and receive it. Hence the alternatives still flourish.

To understand the position of the medical profession and other forms of healing we must examine the past.

[1] *'Qu'est-ce qu'un tyran? Une âme aveugle.'*

A CONDENSED
HISTORY OF MEDICINE

It is often asserted that primitive forms of society practiced healing as an adjunct to religion, and this is superficially true. However, forms of therapy such as psychosomatic medicine and spiritual healing might be regarded in the same way by historians who know less of our current history than we would like to record.

According to archaeological discoveries, in Kenya for example, man would appear to have been on this planet for at least 2,500,000 years. Skilled trephining has been found on skulls buried in the mastaba and pyramids of Egypt. The discovery of radium by the Curies was facilitated by observing a native witch doctor treating sick people by burying them up to their necks in radium-bearing mud.

Medical traditions developed in China, where it became the custom to pay a doctor to keep the patient well, and to stop paying him the moment the patient became ill, a wiser procedure than that which prevailed in the West. Herbalists are still using herbs which this civilization, and other early ones, discovered had therapeutic properties.

In ancient Egypt there was a House of Life attached to the big temples, where people were restored to health, and a House of Death where those about to depart were prepared, as is described in the Egyptian *Book of the Dead,* for their life hereafter. Thoth, also called *Phar Ma Kee,* was the god of healing, and from his name the Greeks took their word *pharmakon,* from which is derived the English words pharmacy, pharmaceutic, etc.

Western tradition stems, naturally enough, from the Greeks, and the knowledge they acquired from their Near East neighbors. Cnidus, on the promontory of Triopium,

Caria, was a colony of Lacedæmonians, famed for holding the Praxiteles statue of Aphrodite. It also had a school of medicine (700–600 B.C.). Here we find the earliest collation of details and rationalizations of symptoms of disease. Since little else remains, we might infer, perhaps unjustly, that the patient seemed to matter less than the disease.

On the island of Cos, one of the Sporades near the Carian coast Hippocrates (c. 460–357 B.C.) established a school of medicine and wrote the books which are still partly extant. Nobody else but Hippocrates, as far as our records show, applied logic and systematization to therapy, symptoms and aetiology. Recent research reveals that this remarkable herbalist discovered many therapeutic specifics over two thousand years ago. Hippocrates was widely acclaimed throughout Greece as a very brilliant physician, and his sons followed his career, also with success. In showing that disease was not the vengeance of the gods, Hippocrates performed a lasting service to mankind. 'The fault, dear Brutus, lies not in our stars, but in ourselves . . .'[1] Hippocrates paid great attention to diagnosis, not only of outward symptoms, but also of the diet and the mental condition of the patient; he was the forerunner of psychosomatic healing too.

We are hampered by difficulties with precise translations of the records of later schools of medicine, and fewer of their textbooks have survived. Of the Alexandrian school, for example, one may say that they were basically empirical in their approach, less concerned with causes than Hippocrates, and blinded by the data of symptoms and the fascination of finding new names for them. (Personally, I have rarely found that any two people with a common cold have identical symptoms.)

In Rome, the medical school substituted a royal flush of theories for facts. Until the time of Claudius Galenus (A.D. 130–201) studying medicine there must have been somewhat confusing. Galen (as he was known), physician to Marcus Aurelius, Commodus and Severus, must have been a very good doctor to survive those quick-tempered emperors. His writings show him to be a practical herbalist, a very pro-

---

[1] Shakespeare, *Julius Caesar*.

found scientist and one of the most learned men of his day. He also wrote many impressive papers on the works of Hippocrates and other sources of medical knowledge. About eighty genuine discourses have come down to us, together with a few of suspect authorship.

Although some other practices were creeping in, medicine was in Roman times basically a blend of herbs, baths (see Water Therapy, Kneipp, Sauna), and some psychosomatic treatment.

Medical traditions passed down through the monasteries and the great Arab schools of medicine, both of which were inspired by the Greeks. While Western thought was becoming waterlogged with legends of saints, and in the search for one panacea (healing everything with one specific), the Muslims established the first universities, and produced such men as Ibn-Sina, whom we call Avicenna (979–1037), one of the greatest physicians and thinkers known to history. His extant works, the *Canon of Medicine* and *Book of Recovery,* are profound and exhaustive proofs of his learning. He was one of the chief founders of the philosophy of medicine, but one needs some knowledge of mathematics, logic, physics and metaphysics, as well as of medicine, to comprehend his writing fully. Among other things he demonstrates that there is seemingly one universal law, innumerable variations upon the theme in every mode of existence, and the ultimately all reality proceeds from the divine Absolute. Averroës (1126–98), more properly Abul-ibn-Roshd, was another brilliant Arab physician.

From this tradition, despite doctrinal difficulties, Arab physicians helped found the medical school of Salerno, the first university in Europe. The Abbess Hildegard von Bingen (*c.* 1100–79) constructed her giant herbal; she also wrote beautiful poems and described mystic visions.

A uniquely controversial figure was Theophrastus von Hohenheim (1493–1541), a Swiss physician of Basel University. He was a herbalist who began to dabble in chemistry and metallurgy. He developed a peculiar doctrine of signatures, by which he claimed that all plants which healed a heart condition would have the sign of a heart on the leaf, flower or bark (see my *Concise Herbal Encyclopedia*). This might contain a germ of truth, though on the face of it, it seems to be exaggerated.

Henry VIII in England personally protected herbalists by a royal charter in 1542. By this time physicians and herbalists were split into two factions, the one keeping entirely to herbs, the other admitting any substance which they believed would heal. Practices such as bloodletting and the use of inorganic metals and minerals sometimes produced cures which were worse to endure than the original disease.

Although it is claimed that William Harvey's (1578–1657) discovery of the circulation of the blood was an advance in medicine, it was rather in fact an advance in physiology, because thus doctors knew more precisely how the body worked. Physiology is a branch of study that is still comparatively neglected in the rush to find new drugs. William Harvey was roundly abused for his work, and was only vindicated after his death. Similarly, the great Flemish anatomist Vesalius (1514–64) was attacked by medical and clerical authorities, but as he was chief physician to the Emperor Charles V he was in a stronger position.

It is important to emphasize at this point where the two best known branches of healing became more distinctly separated. There are fundamental differences in philosophy which have been evolved from alternative answers to questions such as, *What are we healing? Example: a patient, a disease, a symptom, a whole condition. Do we heal by attacking the disease? Or do we strengthen the patient's natural defenses so that they can overcome the disease?*

However much attention and acrimony are wasted, the questions cannot be better understood, moreover solved, by posturing, appealing to authority, Heaven, or anybody who would listen rather than apply hard work to thinking. The Dutch poet Joost van der Vondel (1587–1679) put it like this: 'One can never make something that is evil good with the appearance of law.'[2] Unfortunately many people take doubt as a reflection upon their personal honor, claim privilege, appeal to authority to refute the doubter and miss the point. Such doubt may be a golden opportunity for progress;

[2] *'Men maeckt een quade zaeck met schijn van recht nooit goed.'*

as such it should be examined. In Genesis there is a poignant example of man's tendency to blame others for his mistakes. It ended in tragedy and disaster then; it usually does. The existence of different types of healing should be a source of hope and comfort to the patient, never a source of anxiety to the practitioner of any form of healing. Concern for the welfare of a patient may mislead the well-intentioned, but to feel oneself one's *brother's keeper* does not mean being his dictator.

In modern times the history of medicine is more confusing, particularly in England and America. Vienna, Berlin and Paris also produced mini-pogroms of innovators. Many discoveries have been claimed as advances in medicine when they were, in fact improvements in diagnostic techniques, better knowledge of physiology or anatomy.

In 1863 the association of bacteria with disease was established by Davaine's work on anthrax. In 1882 Robert Koch of Berlin discovered the tuberculous bacillus, and later that of cholera. He received the Nobel Prize for Medicine in 1905. The most significant figure in this new field was Louis Pasteur (1822–95), a teacher of mathematics who was deeply interested in chemistry and physics. He became professor of chemistry at Strasburg (1852), and later at Lille (1854). He demonstrated the existence of micro-organisms in the air, and the health of tissues when protected from them. It was widely advertised that his researches benefited the beer, wine and silk industries, but in recent years facts have disputed this claim. However, Huxley stated that Pasteur's work, assessed in money terms, could have paid off France's war indemnity of 1870. The attention of medical schools was diverted from the whole condition of the patient to the specific condition of bacteria invasion and growth within the patient, but this is hardly the fault of Pasteur, a sincere and revered man of science.

Most people have difficulty in distinguishing theory from fact, and many who professed to follow Pasteur allowed enthusiasm to substitute for real positive knowledge. Beauchamp's claim that bacteria are always present in cases of disease, may carry disease-facilitating conditions but still not be the actual disease, became increasingly adopted by the herbalists and fringe-healing arts, but was neglected by the established medical schools. Analogously, a bankrupt's house may be surrounded by bailiffs who are the effect of his bankruptcy, not the cause; or at a street accident there are usually policemen who are the effect of the event, not the cause.

Lurgan Sahib told Kim that it is more important in this world to know why things happen than how. If research bodies could probe deeper into the *why*, we might learn more about ourselves in conditions of health and sickness. In the past much animosity was kindled by a failure to correlate knowledge accurately, and by a lack of detailed information on a wide scale, easily available. This book may help to fill in the gaps which have existed too long between all branches of those who seek to heal the sick.

We see a significant step forward in the work of Ignazius Semmelweiss (1818–65), the first modern gynecologist, called the savior of mothers on account of his discovery of the cause of puerperal fever (childbed fever), which was lack of hygiene on the part of doctors. He taught that hands and clothes should be clean when attending the delivery of children, and introduced disinfection. He was wickedly persecuted for his daring innovations. However, truth conquers ignorance—eventually.

Many discoveries followed inventions, each of which had some influence upon the philosophy of medicine. Here are some examples. Marshall Hall (1790–1857), a Nottingham-born physiologist, was rejected, reviled and ridiculed, but his work concerning the reflex actions of the spinal cord was finally recognized. Lister, the Essex-born surgeon (1827–1912), developed the use of carbolic acid for sterilizing wounds and instruments. Although nobody would apply carbolic acid to human flesh today, in the chaotic conditions prevailing at that time it was considered a major advance. At least in theory it introduced a perfection of cleanliness technique. Thousands of people owe their lives to Bodington, the reformer who taught that tubercular patients needed fresh, clean air as part of their cure. His medical colleagues execrated him and called him a charlatan, but were later forced to admit that his work was logical and correct.

By the nineteenth century the central core of medical practice had arrogated to itself the sobriquet of orthodox (as if they rejected the *'Filioque'* clause and adhered to the Byzantine Church), and derided all others as charlatans. For the unlearned and unwary, such defamatory abuse sounds impressive, but it neither stifled truth nor established claims which were false.

Patients are as willing to be healed by charlatans as by anybody else, especially if one may be poisoned by the unknown side effects of wonder drugs unforeseen by the workers in the pharmaceutical industry (with the best will in the world). As medicine advances, there is an increasing tendency for the side effects of man-made drugs to become irreversible—all the more so if the patient as a whole is studied less than the disease.

One of the beneficial results of the British colonization of India was the opening up of systematized study of tropical diseases. The first schools were in Hong Kong in 1866 and in London in 1898.

Surgery greatly improved, and necessarily, under the impetus of the First World War. Blood transfusions, and the adoption of techniques such as massage, heat treatment (ultraviolet, infrared, etc.) and nutritional science, have all made a powerful impact upon the medical world. 'It's clever, but is it art?' We are obliged all the same to recognize that none of these treatments, applied by medical schools, answers the leading questions which are the first principles of medical philosophy.

Paul Ehrlich (1854–1915), the discoverer of Salvarsan, won a Nobel Prize for his research in serology. He initiated the theory on the magic bullet, a drug which would harm only the bad guys of the bacterial world existing in each body, and not the good bacteria performing essential functions. Without detracting from the value of his work, it is correct to say that the treatment seems to have been generally applied beyond the specific instances in which it might be effective. His theory became a guiding philosophical fallacy in the application of pharmaceutics to the treatment of the sick. So much so that it has lent itself to ridicule from the other branches of healing whose theses led them to doubt the wisdom of the magic bullet. One analogy used is that Ehrlich's

magic bullet treatment is like casting a bomb into a restaurant
to kill off two wicked waiters, having written their names on
it, and hoping nobody else gets hurt! In practice it is now
widely accepted that, useful and interesting as the theory is,
some cell tissues, some healthy bacteria, always get killed as
well as the alien organisms associated with a diseased condition. An investigation (*Evening Standard,* September 28,
1967) reported that twelve experts who tested 2,241 preparations used by the medical profession found that 42 per cent
failed to give satisfaction (a statistic which means little unless you are a patient upon whom one of the failures was
used). Thus perfect selectivity in drugs has so far avoided us.

A significant advance was made by Sir Alexander Fleming
(Nobel Prize for Medicine, 1945), a brilliant bacteriologist
who during his life (1881–1955) contributed much to our
understanding of the behavior of bacteria. His Penicillin was
developed from a living mold *Penicillum notatum,* and the
basis of the therapy is that the Penicillin inhibits the breeding
of harmful bacteria in the bloodstream, and allows them to be
more easily destroyed by the body defenses. This is a similar
mechanism to the Sulphonamides, discovered by Gerhard
Domagk (1895–1968), who won the Nobel Prize in 1939
for his research.

To use bacterial substances to kill other bacteria was an
imaginative attempt to solve the mysteries of healing. In practice scarcely a decade had passed before it was shown that
Penicillin might in some cases produce sudden death, heart
disease and incurable skin disease. Among the other drugs
Aureomycin has been known to cause liver damage and internal bleeding; Cortisone has been found to bring about kidney
disease, revive latent tuberculosis and even bring about insanity.

By the mid-twentieth century the pharmaceutical industry
was fully geared for the domination of the medical profession. One miracle drug has followed another, with the result
that few hard-working doctors have the opportunity, torn between administrative paperwork, visiting and surgery hours,
to test individually products supposedly recommended or
certified by other doctors. It is easy and unfair to accuse the
doctors of Jekyll and Hyde behavior when we ignore the

pressure, seven days a week with few holidays, trying to heal the constant stream of sick, trying to make diagnoses from patients' blurred accounts of symptoms. If they err, it is by the sin of omission rather than of commission.

Authorities may belittle the work done by Sister Kenny (1886–1952), the much-loved Australian nurse who devoted her life to the unfortunate victims of infantile paralysis (treating them with massage and hot, moist applications).[3] However, the average general practitioner is likely to accept the opinion of authorities because the spirit of inquiry has been trained out of him or drained out of him by overwork. Kenny was reviled as a charlatan, despite the fact that hers was the first successful therapy for these unfortunate patients, and she has not yet been fully vindicated.

[3] See *They Shall Walk* by Kenny and Ostenso (1943). Sister Kenny was one healer who could get the patients to walk and live nearly normal lives again.

3

RESULTS OF ERRORS IN THE PHILOSOPHY OF MEDICINE

Philosophy is what we think, regardless of the depth or thoroughness of our thinking. An idea governs our conduct. If the Angmassalik Eskimos consider it moral to put their old people out on the ice for the bears to eat, those of us who think that old people's homes are the answer may find the Eskimos as immoral as they find us.

In ancient India there was a legend about some kindly monkeys. They saw some fish swimming in the pool beneath them. Moved with their scientific knowledge of what was best for the fish and by the compassion it induced, they took the fish out of the water and placed them high in the trees so that the fish should not drown.

Mankind's problems arise frequently from the ubiquitous Procrustes complex. In the Greek legend Procrustes was the robber of Polypemon who tied his victims to the bed that fitted himself. If the victims were longer than his bed he cut their limbs off to fit it; were they too short, then he stretched them on a rack to fit his bed. In many fields of human thinking we find that few of us are able to accept facts without twisting them to the predigested thinking, creeds, beliefs and theories we have accepted.

It is easy to perceive how novelty may be confused with progress, and how insufficient knowledge of the past may induce me to repeat errors. It is not that history repeats itself, merely that men, failing to learn from history, repeat the same blunders in similar situations.

Philosophy is inextricably bound up with the methods of healing the sick, and as such reflected in the results. 'Never heed the hunter's tears,' runs the Arabic proverb, 'watch his hands!'

Dickson Wright told a British Medical Association scientific meeting in Bristol that every year about 10,000 people in Britain alone die of antibiotic drugs. Some 30,000,000 prescriptions a year are issued for sleeping pills and drugs of a narcotic nature, and about 1,000 people a year die from overdoses of sleeping pills in Britain, and over 10,000 in America. Daily and Sunday newspapers abound with details of tragedies arising from taking the new pharmaceuticals, particularly the antibiotic and Sulphonamide drugs. Ralph Nader (1971) showed that Hexachlorophene, which is used in deodorants, baby soap, talcum powder and other products, has produced cases of severe, irreversible brain damage. We may say that this is an overstatement of a small percentage, but then, your child might be one of that small percentage! It is easy to be objective about remote tragedies. Phenylbutozone has been prescribed by doctors for chronic cases of rheumatism. To what extent it really cures the disease I do not know, but two Oxford scientists proved that it can cause permanent genetic damage to the blood. L. F. Prescott of Aberdeen University found (1966) that thirty-six cases of kidney disease and ten deaths were traceable to popularly recommended pain-relieving drugs. Professor Dunlop of Edinburgh found twenty-four fatal cases of abnormal blood conditions related to doses of Chloramphenicol. A report in *The Guardian* (November 24, 1966) cited a drug, Alpha naphthylamine, in connection with cancer of the bladder.

The world is now all too familiar with the terrible Thalidomide tragedy, but here again statistics mean nothing unless one has personally seen the incredible deformities which these child victims must bear for the whole of their lives. It is not only the feeble flopping appendages that should have been arms (one child I saw had pathetic hands sprouting from his shoulders like the useless wings of a kiwi), the deformed legs and hands, but rather the damaged, ineffective internal organs, the crippled spines and injured brains which have blackened the name of drug therapy. One recalls Pope's immortal words about *'Man's inhumanity to Man.'*

Doctors and laymen alike must think of the goal of healing. Admittedly for many the Hippocratic Oath has less meaning now than when men truly believed in Apollo and

Aesculapius, but its intention is still binding. When we see that several universities have established Chairs of Iatrogenic Medicine (that is, medicine to heal diseases caused by taking other medicine) we have some moral obligation and duty to our species to ask whether the golden road to Samarkand has not turned into the golden bough which Aeneas broke off before he descended into hell. This is not what any of us who heal set out to do, and we have to examine not only conscience but also methods, because such is the universality of ideas nowadays that decisions have increasingly wider implications.

Had Renaissance civilization failed, there were independent civilizations in Peru, China and India which might have survived and elevated mankind. As communications have improved, so diversity has decreased. Drugs made in Basel or New York can be had in any part of the globe for the asking (and payment). In terms of pharmacology this means that a drug like Thalidomide can cause disaster in dozens of countries, and the results may not be noticed until several years have passed. However much we may be promised that there will never be another case like this, the reassurance is as empty as a promise made by the first maker of a bow and arrows that he would never make another.

Machiavelli observed that the appearance of virtue is often as useful as virtue itself. In such countries where the medical profession has become part of the state social-security-medical-aid organization, this means that any doctor who refuses to do *puja* to the pundits of his profession is cast out and prohibited from practicing his healing art. Whether a democratically orientated society can tolerate dictatorship politically or in any institution such as medicine is questionable.

One source of hindrance to the proper spirit of research is the self-righteousness which characterizes many authorities of the established medical schools, and that *charisma* of recognition which they hold as a threat over hard-working general practitioners. My friend Preben Andersen did some research, and he found that originally only the Pope had the legal power to issue any degree for medicine, theology, arts, etc., and that universities have usurped the papal power. However, some seven hundred years of doing this does not seem to have destroyed learning or made it less beneficial.

Christian monarchs and prelates all formerly despised the Muslim, but the richest among them did not hesitate to employ Muslim doctors. So much for recognition! It becomes clear that all is not well in the state of established medicine. In fact it is from many of the sincere general practitioners that most of the criticism comes, rather than from the groups of alternative healing practitioners.

Dr. Andrew Malleson, a former London GP now working in Canada, has written *Need Your Doctor Be So Useless?*, a more controversial challenge to outdated medical orthodoxy than most attacks made from without the profession. Many men who have dedicated their lives to alleviating the suffering of the sick through orthodox medicine are more distressed than lay critics when they learn of a man going to hospital for an appendectomy and being sent home with brain damage, because they know better how such things could be avoided. They are disturbed when it is revealed that some hospitals have been experimenting upon patients without their consent, when for example, Dr. Alexandre admits that his unit took nine kidney transplants from living patients to use for other patients without the consent of patient or relative.

The tendency for pride in technique to supplant the simple desire to heal is bringing disgrace to a profession which has done nothing to deserve such opprobrium. It is unlikely that public confidence will be regained until the profession is able to isolate and disown its more irresponsible technologists.

In January 1973 it was revealed that, according to a report by Jessica Mitford in *Atlantic* magazine, American doctors are using prisoners in forty-four U.S. prisons for medical experiments. When German doctors did this in the concentration camps there was great uproar; the experiments have been described in gruesome details in Dr. A. Mitscherlich's book *The Death Doctors*. This type of experimentation may lead science along the *via dolorosa*,[1] it seems to echo Chesterton's

[1] The name of the road Christ trod on his way to the Crucifixion.

> Reeling, road, a rolling road,
>   and such as we did tread
> The night we went to Birmingham,
>   by way of Beachy Head.

We recall Robert Frost's poem 'The Road Not Taken,' which turned out to be best after all.

The research project which showed that in a given period 20 per cent of Glasgow's children were being given aspirin-type drugs before they were one year old caused considerable alarm among doctors and others because many cases of poisoning from these drugs have been recorded. Within a period of four months in 1967, covered by a Medical Defence Union report, ten patients had been given the wrong operation! In the same year there was a scandal about patients' cards being marked *NTBR* meaning *not to be resuscitated* in the case of their condition worsening. Questions have been raised in Parliament about experiments upon mentally handicapped children with neither the permission nor the cognizance of the children's parents.[2]

In *Human Guineapigs* Dr. Maurice Pappworth, a Harley Street specialist, listed some two thousand experiments upon live patients without their knowledge or consent, some upon babies within hours of their birth and without the knowledge of their mothers. Pregnant women and old people have become familiar targets for the experimenters. Senator Seymour Thaler in 1967 denounced[3] an American hospital for injecting live cancer cells into twenty-one patients without their knowledge; we may here recall the disputed claim that Argentinian doctors murdered the beautiful trade union leader Eva Peron by injecting live cancer cells into her blood. Twenty-one New York hospitals admitted experimenting upon three thousand patients with drugs whose effects were unknown.[4]

A case of five hundred children being injected deliberately with the hepatitis virus has also been recorded. Let us be clear about this. There is an ever growing number of orthodox doctors who know that we must look elsewhere for our research

[2] By Sir Derek Walker Smith and Stephen Swingler.
[3] *Daily Telegraph*, January 12, 1967.
[4] *Observer*, January 29, 1967.

into the methods of healing, and who are disgusted with the dictatorial attitude of their medical leaders about what is research.

Research and progress are both emotive words, but we live in an age when emotive words and slogans can too easily become a substitute for thinking. One late September I was watching television with my hosts in a snug Finnish house. There was a program about the need for *progress* in the Arctic regions. An old Lapp neighbor was present and I remember his sad smile as he said: 'It will be easier for them to become richer, easier for us to become poorer.'

If we look unemotionally at statistics it seems that the amount of progress made from orthodox research barely justifies the expense and suffering it causes. Many of the research scientists in medicine give the impression—in John Webster's words—that the goal is:

> To leave a living name behind,
> And leave but nets to catch the wind.

Dr. Hürzeler, a Swiss dentist of Basel University, through an erudite comparison of the teeth and jawbone of man and apes, demonstrated that whereas man's ancestry parallels the simian line, it is not a direct descent. So for those who infer (directly or by innuendo) that man evolved from monkeys, and that the results of research experiments upon lower mammals can indicate the behavior of drugs upon humans, there is less ground for the assumption than is generally credited. Nevertheless, owing to the direction of medical authorities, vivisection upon living animals without anesthetics grows every year. Buddhists say that being cruel to helpless domestic animals is the first step to becoming indifferent to the sufferings of other humans. Magendie, a noted early experimenter, recorded how he took a household pet dog for research. After much intense pain the dog one day escaped, and instead of running away ran toward him, jumped up and licked his face. Magendie boasted of returning the dog to its cage; later he killed it.

Worse happens in laboratories today in the name of progress, and all is held to be for the good of humanity. In Turkey, under the aegis of Professor Dr. Aygün of Ankara University, most research is done on human cell tissues (for example, scraping of skin, etc.) taken from a patient. In view of the effectiveness of these painless methods, it is to be wondered why the medical profession endures the stigma which vivisection brings to it. Experiments grafting a second head onto a puppy,[5] crushing animal limbs, pouring acid upon eyeballs and injecting strains of diseases into animals which normally never acquire such ailments give us all (many general practitioners of medicine included) grave doubts about the psychological health of the experimenters and those who plan such research as well as about the utility of the work. From J. L. Runeberg I quote: 'Only Death turns away his eyes and weeps.'[6]

The *British Medical Journal* (February 15, 1958) carried a report of animals being radiated with cancer-producing gamma rays for sixteen hours. The idea of seeking a cure by creating (in any form) the disease is odd, and one wonders if this is why the orthodox approach to drug addiction has been to provide further supplies of the narcotic to the addict.

While fairly lucid to a graduate of the classics, the Latin and Greek used in medical terminology annoy the ordinary layman in bed intensely. Some doctors make a mystique out of a diagnosis, calling nose-bleeding *epistaxis* and a cold *coryza*. Others, for example Dr. Axel Munthe (*The Story of San Michele*), may blandly use the term colitis for any condition they cannot diagnose. It reminds me of the secret language which the royalty and courtiers of Madagascar used to speak so that none of the commoners should understand them.

The authorities behind orthodox medicine have done little to better their public image, and their research methods are causing alarm among their rank-and-file general practitioners, and more dismay among their patients.

What is the status and public-relations image of the alternative practitioners?

[5] In 1955 Russian research scientists grafted onto a puppy the head of a freshly killed dog; the bi-capital monster was kept alive two months and then died. See Luke 23:34.
[6] J. L. Runeberg (1804–77) was a Finnish-Swedish poet.

4.

QUACKS,
CHARLATANS AND SAINTS

A lifelong friend of a woman I know died because of this remark: 'It's incurable; the doctor told Mother nothing can be done about it!' Nowadays there is more vitality, less subservience, more combativeness manifested, and people try cheerfully anything that has achieved a reputation for healing. Moreover, many people will feel rapport between themselves and some unorthodox healer, and will become cured by him when all else has failed.

It is no longer practical or helpful to the sick for people who hold positions of responsibility and authority to pontificate and damn all those who are not of their own persuasion.

It is true that a number of unfortunate events have brought some alternative healing arts and sciences less repute than many of them deserve. Much of the criticism has been from sincere, honest men suspecting or discovering less honesty among others than they would wish for.

In historical times, and maybe in our own, the trend has been to regard the little that we know as the sum total of knowledge. 'I have found a piece of turmeric,' said the rat, 'I will open a grocer's shop.' While it is embarrassing to read the back issues of old newspapers in which orthodox medical researchers have claimed to have answered all humanity's problems with drugs whose names have been forgotten in a year or two, it is no less edifying to see how some practitioners of alternative healing allow imagination and enthusiasm to make up for lack of knowledge and experience.

The word 'quack' (or quacksalber) has its etymology in two Dutch (and Low German) words: *kwakkelen,* a verb meaning to be sick or ailing, and the other a noun *zalver,* meaning a man who saved or healed (in ecclesiastical circles a priest who anoints the sick). Thus its meaning is 'a healer of the sick,' and has nothing to do with the sound that ducks make. The Saxon word was *cwic,* from which comes the phrase 'the quick and the dead' (the healthy, live people and the defunct). As the Germanic races were conquered or influenced by Latin culture and Christianity, the meaning of many old words deteriorated. For example, Hell (*hel*) was not a place of torment for the tribes, but corresponded with what we understand by Heaven; only warriors went to Valhalla. As Christian monks settled, concepts changed.

The word 'charlatan' relates to a medieval Italian root, meaning one who claims a lot more than he can accomplish. However, in view, for example, of the connection of Phenacetin with some cases of kidney disease (first reported from Stockholm) one wonders where charlatanry ends and mere errors in research begin.

The disapproval of medical treatment was first recorded, I believe, by St. Bernard of Clairvaux (1091–1153), a devout man who wrote beautiful hymns but was not renowned for tolerance, and who seems to have regarded it sinful for his monks to practice healing because sickness was a punishment for sins. He was also responsible for the persecution of Abélard, lover of Héloïse. The Middle Ages abounded with dirt and malnutrition, and consequently with sickness, plague and diseases. The economic chaos, continual wars and insecurity made the people selfish and indifferent to the sufferings of others. Throughout Europe semiliterates would wander, selling cures, relics of the Rood on which Christ died and anything else—for money.

It becomes difficult to distinguish in history the true and the false; there is not so much distinct black and white as a mingling of grays.

How some herbalists, such as Culpeper, managed to rise above the corruption around them, even by the seventeenth century, excites admiration, particularly when they lost business and reputation by trying to help the poor.

The eighteenth century and the first part of the nineteenth century were famed for the proliferation of unorthodox healers. 'Spot' Ward with his cure-all pills became a royal favorite of George II, and a remarkably wealthy man. Hill, who made his fortune from selling an infallible remedy for gout, was unable to save his own life with the same medicine, since he is said to have died following a severe attack of gout. John Case, John Taylor Brodnum (infallible cure for venereal diseases), James Graham and others preyed viciously upon the credulity of the public and upon the purses of the rich.

However this was an age of enlightenment and there was a demand for reason. Ever since the French Revolution, edicts had obliged men and women to seek logic rather than legends. While self-sacrifice did not flourish overnight, many alternative healing practitioners began to emerge as healers in their own right, with a code of charging those who could afford to pay for treatment, and healing the poor free. Mrs. Mapp, the bone-setter from Epsom, Surrey, died in poverty owing to her devotion to healing, although her sister married a duke!

Samuel Hahnemann taught homeopathy, and the great German reformers of diet, advocates of baths, water, air and sunshine healing were at work. Samuel Thomson (1769–1843), father of modern herbalism, Coffin and Tilke (his disciples) brought a totally new concept to the entire idea of healing: no toxic substance was to be used. The herbalists were the first (and until now still the sole) doctors to reject the use of any drug, which could possibly harm a healthy body, being used to cure the sick.

The main criticism of the non-established healers is that they have worked for money alone, with little regard for the welfare of their patients. An *Observer* report (February 12, 1967) described one orthodox doctor who made $500,000 a year from forty abortions a week. My point is that making money, even exorbitantly, is a human failing, and not related to the validity of a science or art. The unworthiness of a priest, says the Catholic Church in its wisdom, by no means affects the worthiness of a sacrament he administers. I think the time has come to apply this verdict to healers, all kinds of healers.

DIAGNOSIS IN DISPUTE

A more common criticism of the practitioners of alternative healing is that they have not studied diagnosis sufficiently to be reliable therapists. I have said before that any fool can discover a fact, but it takes a genius to interpret it. We are short of genius. Diagnosis is the identification of a disease by means of its symptoms, which sounds very well until you learn that there are dozens of conditions which have virtually identical symptoms as classified by the orthodox or allopathic (the adjective used by homeopaths) school of medicine. Naming a condition is easier than curing it, but if we try to identify every variation of every known condition, students might have to spend longer learning this than learning to heal the illness.

Healing is a very simple process if you know what is wrong with the patient. This, as Hippocrates taught, is the quintessence of therapy. As one Harley Street specialist has put it, there are no diseases, only sick people. The trouble with diagnosis which relies upon the patient's description is that most people are unable to describe their complaint in medical terms, and are often in too much pain (or under nervous stress) to tell the healer small details. Radionic diagnosis eliminates this, but not everybody learns to handle the diagnostic computer correctly. The true herbalist cannot work from the same type of diagnosis as the allopath because his conception of illness is totally different. He must not ask himself which germs or virus have attacked this body, but which organs and systems of this body are failing in their function so that they no longer resist as they should this alien development.

Chiropractors, osteopaths, masseurs, etc., make diagnoses

frequently from X rays, but acupuncturists and dietitians have little use for that approach. It is useless to insist upon all practitioners of healing receiving the same sort of initial training in diagnosis, because the theories of healing frequently diverge significantly from those held by the established schools of medicine.

I was recently asked what on earth philosophy has to do with medicine. Far more, I fear, than has been widely accepted, for in the differences of thought patterns the lives and health of millions of people are at stake.

The human race can only survive if the stock is basically healthy. Fertility is one of the first victims of disease. My Italian professor in classical history told me that it has been established that the health, mental vigor and fertility of the early Romans was undermined by the use of lead for piping water supplies, cooking utensils, etc. Lead is toxic.

According to the orthodox system of diagnosis it may become more difficult to link ill health with simple causes, because this system is by its very nature more concerned with effects than prime causes. It tends to ask what germs have we here, instead of why are these germs here, how did they thrive in the body.

At one time infantile paralysis was linked with sea bathing and even indoor swimming pools. It was discovered that many seaside resorts deposited their towns' sewage too short a distance out at sea, whence the tide swept it back in again. In the latter case more rigid rules about swimmers and bathers taking a proper shower before entering public baths have been adopted. Links between excreta and polio have been established.

If we know, philosophically, what we are healing, then we can direct our energies to the source of the illness. Otherwise it is like duck shooting at night with a blindfold over our eyes.

Unfortunately, revising our ideas about diagnosis emphasizes how little we know compared with how much we thought we knew.

THE SEARCH FOR A BALANCE

Hitherto antipathy between branches of healing has hindered them from exchanging ideas and learning from each other. I want this book to provide an impetus for healers of all kinds to come together in a democratic way, not to settle their differences, but to see how they can achieve a meeker attitude to research and the fundamental goal of healing the sick for the sake of the patients. Professional pride has never yet healed any sick man or woman. Academic, verbal pyrotechnics consume time and energy which should be devoted to the study of logic.

At one time I attended the lectures of Professor Wilhelm Emrich, the world's greatest authority on Kafka. Neither years in a Nazi concentration camp nor the threats of Ulbricht's Communist regime ever silenced his determination to speak the truth; it was, he said, the best way to serve humanity.

Credo quia absurdum,[1] Tertullian's famous remark, is no longer valid. One of the difficulties of navigation is that yawing to one degree is enough to lead a boat farther away from its destined port the longer it travels on a false course. The population explosion and other factors make it more imperative that we should find, and hold on to, a correct, balanced course.

The physical, economic and psychological factors of late twentieth-century life differ from those of urban life in other centuries. The outbreak of an epidemic in some Asiatic town may spread very fast owing to the speed of transport, movement of travelers, goods, etc. This is one reason why all those

---

[1] I believe it because it is absurd.

whose sincere interest is healing should get together and examine all the known methods of healing. The examination will have to be made by those who have no vested interests in any particular system, because that can unduly distort a man's judgment. Such an investigation should be made by people without a direct emotional involvement in one or another school of therapy, so that there is clarity of thought. Too often allopaths scoff at a method of healing because it is incongruous within their own concepts, rather like a maker of sundials telling a clockmaker that his watch cannot work because it is not made of the right stone.

The orthodox critics of other types of healing lead us to infer that everybody is a scoundrel outside their ranks, that other systems of healing must be fraudulent. Their training does not, however, concern itself as much with morality as does theological instruction. However, even churches have their failures, so medical dogma may be set aside in the search for balanced healing.

It was the custom of medieval university training to teach scholars logic, and to treat other subjects as of secondary importance. In a pragmatic, business-dominated civilization such as ours, it is facile to claim that we have no time for such abstruse studies. Ecologists are saying that man as a species may have less time left on this planet than we think if we cannot re-educate our scientists to seek a symbiosis rather than assume domination of this planet.

Human conceptions of morality vary, but there are some universal truths which do not alter with circumstances or vary with political opinions: water wets us, fire burns; whereas goodness may turn sour and produce evil, it is seldom that evil can be said to produce goodness.

If our philosophical concepts of healing exclude the great spiritual realities of life, they will necessarily bring more harm than healing to the patient and practitioner alike. So very often in the history of medicine the remedy has been both available and obvious, but the way in which it has been sought has been too difficult for man to find. 'Get me 300 milch bats to make possets to procure sleep' cries the doctor in Webster's *Duchess of Malfi*. Three centuries later people still pour quantities of pills and bizarre mixtures down their

gullets in search of sleep. Many of them merely suffer from a
deficiency of mineral salts which could be remedied by drinking a large spoonful of pure honey in warm (not hot) milk.

The original inhabitants of Easter Island ran the entire
gamut of therapeutics, using only three herbs singly or in
combination. Modern man is so inundated with drugs that
few doctors can keep pace with the continual stream of pharmaceutical products advertised. Unless our bodies have
changed very considerably or new diseases are being created
(if so, how? by us? by our misuse of environment and ecology?) then we are entitled to doubt whether the avenues of
research are leading to any positive results. If new diseases
are being created they must have origin. By eradicating them
we destroy the source and thus the diseases. By exploring
hitherto neglected ideas of healing, however old they may be,
we can perhaps gain a new perspective which will enlighten
us as to the nature of disease.

7

ANTIQUITY AND PROGRESS

All I had wrought I abandoned to
  the faith of the faithless years.
Only I cut on the timber—
  only I carved on the stone:
After me cometh a Builder.
  Tell him, I too have known.

History and archaeology constantly remind us that ours is
neither the sole sophisticated generation nor the wisest. The
Greek myths contain lessons in psychology which are so advanced that only now can we begin to understand what they
signify. To understand how advanced some of our primitive
forefathers were, let us consider a few isolated facts. In the
National Museum in Baghdad are objects nearly four thousand years old identified as portable electric cell batteries.
Professor Farrington showed that the ancient Greeks were
using jet propulsion (in steam) some twenty-five hundred
years ago. Diodorus of Sicily (first century B.C.) accurately
describes the coast of America, lying so many days' journey
west of Africa. By mathematics and knowledge of optics the
Greeks were able to create illusions of perspective in the
Parthenon (450 B.C.). Are we justified in assuming that
these intelligent people were stupid when it came to medicine?

Let us look at *Urtica dioica* which the Romans, in particular, used against chills, feverish colds, bleeding, bladder troubles, skin diseases and as a spring tonic. It has been shown to
contain silica, calcium, chlorophyll, vitamins A and C, iron, a
substance similar to histamine, formic acid and a glucose similar to quinine. It is the common stinging nettle!

ant, *Achillea millefolium,* reputed to have been
by that Achilles whom Homer made immortal, is
heal wounds, to treat asthmatic conditions, for
a, for fevers, heart troubles, etc. It contains volatile
(cineol, etc.), bitters and many other curative proper-
s, and is far safer to use than quinine. It is yarrow, a plant
egarded as a weed by the unwise!

The difficulty in distinguishing between what is novel and
what is progress has led many enthusiasts to 'throw the baby
out with the bath water.' During the Second World War the
Germans ran their hospitals and domestic surgeries on drugs
made from herbs which grew in the countryside, which were
collected and dried by schoolchildren, and which cost the
state absolutely nothing. How lucky for the taxpayers! This
work gave a boost to the interest in historic remedies, especially herbal.

If we take the trouble to read the fascinating descriptions
of early voyagers, such as Lewis and Clark's expedition to
the Rockies (1804–6), or the narratives of Sven Hedin
(1865–1952) about Khorasan and wildest Turkestan, one
is struck by the fact that the explorers knew where they
were going and what they were looking for. However, the
search for progress in human health gives one a grave sensa-
tion of vagueness. It might not be wholly without foundation
to say that man probably knows more facts about the planet
than he does about his own body and its functions.

If our definitions are clear-cut, our reasoning will be
clearer, and if we are to make real, as distinct from advertised, progress in the field of healing the sick, then we must
all put more hard work into thinking than hitherto. As a
young man, I knew Sonia Arova, the Bulgarian-born ballerina; her dancing and her success were both phenomenal.
We were good friends, and she used to tell me often that her
achievements were the result of hard work, that there is no
substitute for hard work; if you work hard and put your heart
and mind to your task, nothing can ever stop you being a success. How right she was.

I recently visited a learned friend of mine who was com-
plaining of feeling unwell. I suggested that I should go into
his garden and look for some herbs which might help him. As

I left the back door of the house I slipped in some water. I noticed that the drain below his kitchen window had become blocked up; not only was it flooding, it was stinking! Such a simple thing, so easily overlooked, may facilitate the development of ill health. We quickly cleared the drain, washed ourselves thoroughly, and made a cup of tea. I didn't prescribe any herbs for my friend that day. As I confidently expected, his condition cleared up within twenty-four hours—the cause had gone. So much ill health is caused by dirt, rubbish, neglect and the conditions arising from these.

I remember some of the villages between Skopje and Prizrn in the old days; the piles of rotting melon rinds and horse dung would be black with flies, which would move only to settle upon the tired, dried-looking slabs of red meat in the open stalls which passed for butchers' shops.

Harry Benjamin, world-famous naturopath, wrote: 'After nearly a hundred years of adherence to the germ theory . . . disease exerts as firm a hold upon humanity as heretofore. The germs appear to thrive better than their victims.'

Part of my academic life was spent in Copenhagen where fishmongers kept live fish swimming in a tank of regularly changed sea water. I feel sick when people lay long-dead fish on cold slabs and allow dust and flies to get at them before eating it.

We cannot heal safely or efficiently unless we know the true nature and origin of disease. If we gave more attention to teaching cleanliness and self-discipline, and ate naturally pure foods, we could do much to eradicate many of the diseases which exist around us. It is not enough to concentrate our ideas of cleanliness upon killing germs; we must make clean bodies a universal habit. One of the objections of the Cheyenne to white missionaries and their insistence upon clothing the body, was that, once clothed, the palefaces didn't wash their bodies.

In my youth I would dive into the Rhine and swim manfully against the current, loving the struggle, emerging breathless but triumphant. Now, man-made chemicals have turned it into the sewer of Europe, and the same may be said about many rivers and lakes all over the world! Read Fenimore Cooper's description of the Great Lakes, Erie especially; you

cannot recognize them. To swim in such water is so dangerous that a stomach pump must be used upon those who acci-
dentally do. However much it is filtered, this water has none
of the taste, cleansing properties and mineral salts found in
pure, natural waters.

The answer does not lie in artificially sterilized, antiseptic
precautions. According to experiences in Sweden and the
United States, children who are shielded from all possible
contacts with germs respond by falling seriously ill to the first
bacteria invasion of their system, dying of ailments such as
measles, influenza, etc.

I remember my grandparents' generation most vividly. Illness was exceptionally rare. They breathed unpolluted air.
They drank pure, unpolluted water, not urban sewage three
times processed. They ate foods which were fresh, simple and
nourishing. Their diet was not monotonous; they flavored it
with mineral- and vitamin-rich herbs collected free from
hedgerows and meadows, putting tansy in their buns, thyme in
their pastry, etc. Nobody had sprayed their crops with poisons
to kill the insects, for then there were more birds than now to
keep down insects for nothing.

(Rachel Carson's *Silent Spring* gives statistics of the myr-
iads of birds killed by using DDT and similar chemical
sprays.) My grandparents rose early in the morning, went to
bed early, were full of fun and vitality. Morfar (my
mother's father) could walk at eighty as sprightly and as far
as I could at eighteen, and I was no slouch. And we think
we've got progress? There were, it is true, not many hospitals,
no socialized medicine as now, and no punitive taxes extorted
to pay for them. As Samuel Lover's Handy Andy put it:
'There's people dying now that never died before.'

Man has so altered his environment and damaged the ecology in vast areas of the world that it is doubtful whether any
generations after my own will see Europe as once Ulysses saw
it. I am of the last generation of Europeans who remember
the world before the universal introduction of a motorcar. As
a child I was taken out into the garden to look at an airplane,
such a curiosity it then was!

'We are not lost,' said an old American Indian, 'we are
here, it is the camp that is lost.' Brantridge had as its aca-

demic motto the following gem: 'Wisdom not violence' (*Sapientia non violentia*). This is, I think, the particular goal which mankind has lost. Our general attitude to the earth and all that lives and grows upon it is one of violent demand rather than of seeking intelligent cooperation with the basic realities of life. The number of human beings on the planet is multiplying too quickly. We need more foodstuffs and raw materials for them. Fallacies and traditional taste habits lead us to adopt diets which create an excessive demand for one type of food, for example, wheat, beef, etc. Other crops such as millet and rye often grow more easily and abundantly than wheat. The exterminators of the American buffalo found that European-exported cattle neither fared as easily nor fattened as quickly on the prairie grasses. Early writers such as Charles Sealsfield (born Karl Postl in 1773, in Popitz, Mähren) who wrote *Die Prairie am Jacinto,* describe it so well.

Our solution hitherto has been to try to force the earth to produce more by use of man-made chemical fertilizers. There is weighty evidence that crops are neither as nutritious nor of such natural high yield as they once were. Over a hundred million pounds of artificial, man-made pesticides have been deposited on the earth, cast upon the waters and sprayed into the air. Tobacco crops are sprayed with arsenical preparations, and arsenic is a known carcinogen (cause of cancer). An eminent biologist has published a paper warning us that soon man may no longer be able to eat fish from the sea owing to the astronomically large amount of chemicals being deposited yearly into the oceans. Chemicals such as DDT and chlorinated hydrocarbons are insoluble in rain water, but they do dissolve dangerously in human fats. The human nervous system needs fats for its natural insulation; if the body is starved of them (as during slimming courses worked out by amateurs) the patient becomes irritable, as the nerves lack sufficient fats to make up natural replacements for their fatty sheathing insulation. If these chemicals begin to permeate the fats, and dissolve in them, the damage to the human nervous system may well prove beyond repair. The use of artificial fertilizers and pesticides kills off worms and moles, which are essential to the aeration of the soil. (Moles churn up a very fine-quality, pest-free soil.)

The advent of the car has meant that the soil has been depleted of the natural dung of horses, which are now less profitable to breed, because of the fall in demand for them. This does sound like the enthusiastic Scot in Surtees' (1803–64) *Jorrocks, Jaunts and Jollities* crying: 'Muck's your man!' But the dung of cattle, horses, sheep and even of rabbits, contains a natural balancer that no artificial manure does.

An ancient Chinese saying was that medicine is needed only when food has failed. We know that the quality of our food has changed. We know that most people are eating more carbohydrates than protein. Crop farmers managed to persuade the authorities that corn was more needed than animal proteins, so man proceeded to kill off rabbits because they ate too much corn. Rabbits are the cheapest source of protein; in my boyhood a full-grown rabbit only cost 10¢! Of course the human body can make carbohydrates from excess of protein, but it cannot make excess carbohydrates into proteins. The Nazi concentration camp doctors conducted experiments which proved that people on a high-carbohydrate diet were easier to govern than those on a high-protein diet; interesting, isn't it?

All of this information directly affects the individual, particularly in the light of the fallacy that bacteria are the sole cause of disease. There is now a vast gap between food and nutrition. Unless man begins to think in global fashion about his food supplies and the quality of foodstuffs (instead of mere bulk), we may find that flesh of our bodies becomes increasingly host to more ills, bacteria, etc. As Kipling put it:

> As was the sowing, so the reaping
> Is now and evermore shall be.
> Thou art delivered into thine own keeping.
> Only Thyself hath afflicted thee!

8

A WAY FORWARD

I believe we are entering upon an age of awareness when men all over the world are becoming conscious of a need for enlightenment, and alive to the alternatives that await us (*facilis descensus averno*) should we fail.

Authority is being questioned more than ever before during the last two millennia. I believe that from a spirit of inquiry disciplined by logic, and by a sincere spirit of good will, all practitioners of healing can put together the facts known and arrive at a better understanding of health and sickness in human life.

What we really know, in contradistinction to what fits our theories, is not much, but some facts are fairly solid. Firstly, disease as a dangerous entity does not exist unless found in contact with a sentient being (human, animal, etc.). Even anthrax does not harm anthrax, however lethal it is to sentient beings (particularly humans). Too little research has been conducted on the lines of what renders a sentient being suitably conditioned for the development of disease.

Secondly, neither plants nor animals flourish in conditions that are wholly hostile to them. This appears to be the same for virus and bacterial life forms. A little research has been done along these lines. We know that some bacteria feed upon others, and may prevent their development and multiplication. It is likely that invading organisms destroy bacteria which would, if the body were in a state of good health, hinder their progress.

Thirdly, we accept that good health is a normal, positive condition for humans and animals, and that departures from this are negative in that they detract from the efficiency and comfort associated with good health. By learning to repolarize the negative into positive channels we can learn to make conditions insalubrious for organisms not associated with positive good health.

Fourthly, in the field of nature, generally speaking it is the unhealthy that fall prey to their predators. Fungi, which we may equate with virus, and insects, which we may liken to bacteria, always attack unhealthy plants rather than healthy ones. Seals are known to attack only unhealthy fish, although certain of the fur interests whose concern with culling seals is suspect would have us believe otherwise. Lions, leopards and even foxes, run down the unhealthy specimens of those upon which they prey.

Professor Stackpoole O'Dell demonstrated in his lectures that this entire universe is a theme and variations, a doctrine similar to Avicenna's. Man does not exist in total isolation from the world about him, and his physical body is subject to its physical rules.

9.

MIND AND HEALTH

Our explorations into the field of health and sickness in relationship to the human body have shown us one ray of light, deceptive rather than obvious: the sick must desire healing before they can be healed. Case-history files and experience show all those engaged in healing that some patients use sickness, consciously or otherwise, as a punishment of the body, as self-inflicted hate, a symbol of frustration or as a social excuse. In many cases there is some situation or conditions which the mind cannot face up to, and sickness of varying intensity, seriousness and duration ensues. Unfortunately, an untrained mind may set a ball rolling which it cannot control and may not be strong enough to reverse.

Bacteria are often blamed for our ills instead of the conditions which are the result of the way we live. When the American Indians began to die out on the crowded, insanitary reservations, missionaries and others ascribed this to their sinful ways rather than to the starvation of the people by those who had promised to feed them—if only they would lay down their arms.

Sometimes the human mind believes what it wants to believe, because it is easier to accept than the stark realities of human stupidity and perversity. In Tokyo the stench of chemicals has so ruined the air that clever men have made machines which supply pure oxygen through masks to the affluent citizens who can afford them. Even Madrid, famed by poets for centuries for its beautiful air, has fallen victim to industrial smoke pollution. In eastern Norway and western Sweden snow has fallen, blackened by chemical dust and poisons. Until we prevent conditions such as these, the ever-increasing taxes to pay for more socialized medical services and drugs will more likely reach the point of inducing economic chaos than better health.

It would greatly help our understanding of health if we could accept that the great, open world in which we live is not our enemy but our friend, and it is we who must learn to live with and within it. No marriage can survive if one partner sets out to dominate the other by brute force. Man is married to the earth, but has not learned to live with it. Past errors hang around our neck like Coleridge's albatross, and we must master the art of living within our own environment in a way that does not harm the conditions of ecological balance of plant, air and water especially, for ourselves, and more important for those who come after us, our inheritors, the children whose lives must be spent in the conditions of health and sickness we create for them. Perhaps it is not too much to hope for that we may give this some precedence over our journey to conquer distant stars and planets.

In a plot of land of a square mile there average twenty-five million insects and the amount of airborne bacteria over such an area defies counting; it is legion. Each has some purpose in ecology and the balance of life, for us as well as for other life forms. Truly, as Heraclitus of Ephesus (540–480 B.C.) taught, all things are moving. As you read this, new galaxies are being formed in outer space, and beneath us and around us the universe teems with life forms. If our only method for healing the sick is to be the compilation of catalogues classifying which bacteria are found in which specific cases of sickness, may the task not be beyond our capacity? If the causes are deeper than the presence of bacteria, then it is high time we examined them.

Many of the alternative types of healing included in this work indicate that the cause of disease does lie deeper than the alien organisms which are found, and we do less than justice to ourselves and posterity if we fail to examine these systems and try them, as we feel moved, in the search of truth.

Part two

THE
GUIDE TO ALTERNATIVE
MEDICINE

1.

ACUPUNCTURE AND MOXIBUSTION

This is one of the finest contributions made by the Chinese to the science and art of healing, but to some it seems incomprehensible. One thing is, however, certain: acupuncture effects cures where many other systems cannot. The nearest we get to a better understanding of it is through RADIESTHESIA (*q.v.*).

The system acquired fame in the West about the middle of this century through the press. The first reports came from those who had lived in China, Hong Kong, Singapore, etc. Acupuncture is nearly as old as herbalism in Chinese medical history. Both are twenty-five times more ancient than the allopathy which poses as orthodox medicine today.

The theory is that there are meridian lines which pass through the body that are quite distinct from the actual physical nervous system of man, and they convey a mind force or life force (translation from Chinese is usually vague for abstract ideas). This force must function without any hindrance for bodily health to be maintained.

The healer takes needles of pure copper, gold or silver and inserts them lightly in the flesh at specific points along the lines of the meridians (of which more later). The needles generally penetrate just below the skin, and with a good therapist there is virtually no discomfort at all. The needle sets up a current of impulse along the line of the meridian, which goes to the central nervous system and causes a corresponding effect in the organ or part of the body which is out of balance. The system works, however incredulous the inexperienced may feel about it; acupuncture is eminently successful.

A deciding factor is the expertise of the practitioner in

finding an exact spot along the specific meridian. Such techniques cannot be learned by cramming a few pages of a textbook to memory and hoping to get a passing mark at examinations. Mastering the position and progression of meridian lines takes years of practical experience. To find the exact points along any one meridian demands a natural, radiesthesic sense, and a very long period of training under the tuition of a master of the art. Allopaths tend to call this unscientific. So perhaps we might call sailing unscientific. Ask yourself if you would rather set to sea, trusting your life to a man who has spent many years learning his knowledge of the sea from a master mariner, or risk your life with one who had read it all up in books. There are some branches of knowledge that no acquaintance with books can ever teach us. Would those who doubt this read a book on rock climbing and go at once up the north face of the Eiger?

Some human beings who are more radiesthesically sensitive than others have explained that they can sense a small nodule of power at the exact place of a meridian point. Even so, such ability in detection requires a long period of practical experience. A doctor from Seoul who has spent a lifetime researching into this science has built a machine which uses electricity to speed up the identification of the points and meridians, but this is not universally accepted. Many still regard the millennia-old pulse detection method more accurate.

For Westerners versed in medicine, taking a pulse to measure the speed of the heartbeat and consequent blood circulation is the nearest approximation of the method. The acupuncturist searches out the vibrations given off by a specific point, although he might not use exactly that phrase to describe the process. Three fingers are generally used for this method of taking the pulse.

The Communist government of China is certainly convinced that Nei Ching is effective, and have given their official blessing to acupuncture. The ancient emperors, also, did much to encourage efficiency among practitioners; they cut off the heads of those who failed to heal. To put this in a proper perspective we must remember that the old system was that people had regular check-ups before they became ill. It was then easier for symptoms and conditions to be detected and put right before serious damage developed.

In the purely prophylactic and protective capacity, acupuncture is remarkably good. But too often people go to alternative healing arts only after all allopathic efforts have failed. Too much time has been lost, and many cases are far advanced and more difficult to cure completely.

Behind most Chinese forms of therapy lies the concept of positive and negative, or *Yang* and *Yin* (both words may be translated in several different ways). The Chinese claim that in all diseases the balance of the two forces is out of true. The twelve meridians convey both deep energy and superficial energy as a manifestation of the *Yang* and *Yin* forces, neither of which is ever entirely pure, since all *Yang* contains some degree of *Yin*, and vice versa. The method is far more complicated for the true Chinese-style acupuncturist, since a totally different system of diagnosing diseases is involved. To start with, the terms 'positive' and 'negative' are generally translated as being male and female, although this misleads us as to the scope of the original Chinese. Then there are further classifications according to the traditional five basic patterns, which have been translated as wood, water, metal, earth and fire. For general work there seem to be 365 different points along the twelve meridian lines, and the pattern's resemblance to days and months of the year is noticeable.

In China, the removal of brain tumors and thyroid, correction of pressure by spinal vertebra on spinal-cord nerves, gastric operations and several deaf-mute cures, all solely by acupuncture, were recorded by Winston S. Churchill, M.P., in an account of what he had seen during his visit to China in an article in the London *Observer* (April 30, 1972). Some cases of hernia being cured are also known.

There is a unique feature of acupuncture which I must describe. When a patient has the needles inserted correctly he can calmly watch the surgeons cut away part of his stomach during an operation, and a woman may watch her child being born. This is because acupuncture obviates the need for any anesthetics. There are no noxious potions, nothing to upset the patient, and since no messages of pain have been tearing down to the brain from an outraged nervous system, there are no after-effects at all. The patient just begins to feel better. Some have been known to eat fruit during an operation on the spine!

Acupuncture is one of the most amazing branches of healing. In case anybody doubts the existence of the meridians, I am informed that the Chinese have managed to prove their existence both by electronic aids and by a specialized form of photography.

Moxibustion

This is another form of therapy that has come to us from the Far East. It comprises a token form of burning, often effected with leaf-down from wormwood or sunflower pith, although cotton wool has been used occasionally.

The principles of application are almost identical to those of acupuncture. Hitherto there is comparatively little reliable literature on this art, and I have been unable to trace any authoritative body such as exists for many forms of healing. It is reported to be as efficacious as acupuncture itself.

2.

THE ALEXANDER METHOD

Frederick Matthias Alexander was born in 1869 in Tasmania and died in London in 1955. During his lifetime he formulated and developed a theory that has become known as the Alexander Method. This method, which is increasingly being accepted by medical, educational and psychiatric workers, states that a great deal of modern man's illness can be traced to the way in which he uses his body; muscles are tense when they should not be; backs are "humped," vertebrae contracted together; the neck is sunk into the chest; legs are constantly crossed and toes turned in, tensing and straining all the muscles from the hips. These tensions greatly contribute to many of the complaints now common in contemporary society, such as arthritis, back pain, slipped discs, rheumatism, fibrositis and a great variety of nervous diseases.

The Alexander Principle propounds that in the conditions of modern stressful life we have lost the natural use of our bodies, taking on, often in early childhood, bad habits of posture and movement copied from our elders. These habits are so ingrained that when we are shown the correct use of our bodies, it seems "wrong" to us. The Alexander Method therefore involves a course of retraining pupils in correct use of their bodies by carefully trained teachers.

Alexander developed his method by working on himself. He had lost the use of his voice on which he depended as an actor, and found no help from a number of doctors. By experimenting in a mirror, he discovered that he could stop making certain muscular tensions in his neck which were affecting the functioning of his voice. In the process, not only did his vocal trouble disappear, but he discovered that the way he was using the rest of his body was also affecting the way the rest of his body worked. He found that this principle could be applied to many "stress" diseases such as high blood-pressure and digestive trouble, as well as to the many states of anxiety and depression which civilized life may produce.

He settled in London in 1904 and in the next twenty years developed his concept of "use." His book *The Use of the Self*, aroused considerable interest on the part of doctors and teachers and he attracted many pupils in the 1930s, among them George Bernard Shaw, Aldous Huxley, Professor John Dewey, Stafford Cripps and Archbishop William Temple. In 1973, when Professor Tinbergen was given the Nobel Prize for Medicine, he devoted a major part of his Nobel oration to Alexander's work. These teachers are welcomed in state schools in London where educational authorities have recognized the importance of teaching correct "use" to children before the bad habits they pick up from their elders have become ingrained.

The Alexander Method is not a form of physiotherapy. It is a demanding approach to personal living which leads, through voluntarily accepted discipline, to a personal freedom and health that is possible to some extent for most people at most ages. It demands a willingness to work on oneself, to refine one's attention, in order to become aware of tensions and of "wrong use."

3.

AIR THERAPY

Some decades ago I went on a camping expedition with a friend. Mine was the part to go first, erect the tent, have a meal hot and ready and wait for the friend who was unavoidably coming by a later train (and thence walking) to the site.

It rained solidly and continuously from the moment I left London and long after I erected the walled 'A' tent in a corner of heathland in Hardy's Wessex.

I was soaked to the skin, shivering, and put on a lot of extra clothing, with the disastrous result that I found my sinus playing up and symptoms of a cold developing alarmingly. But I was determined not to spoil a jolly good outing for a thing like that. I sat there and thought how the symptoms had arisen, why they had arisen, what I had done that could make them feel worse. I was cooking the meal over a stove in the tent; it was a good tent, warm and dry, although only of treated, thin cotton.

Moved by inspiration, I took off some clothing, sat in an open-necked shirt and jeans. Within ten minutes my symptoms and discomfiture had gone entirely, and never came back. I did not catch cold at all. The weather turned for the better, and the rest of the Easter outing was perfect. I had learned a lesson that I never forgot. The human body can adjust to almost any one temperature, but it is not built to adapt to varying degrees of heat in various parts. If you muffle yourself up to the neck in thick woolens but leave the face, hands and feet relatively uncovered, you are demanding that your body achieve different temperatures to react to totally different conditions. To absorb oxygen through the skin, the body must open the pores of the skin in the thickly covered areas; so as not to let out too much heat from the uncovered areas, the body normally tries to close the pores of the skin—and all of this at once?

Firstly, being a little cold is different from being wet. Coldness is not so harmful as the damp. Keep dry, but do be careful not to stifle the pores of the skin. Experience has convinced me that artificial man-made fibers are less healthy when worn next to the skin than natural fibers, such as wool and cotton. Most people wear far too much clothing. I am not in favor of nudism, since most people neglect their bodies to the point that they are hideous to look at. Some people, indeed, so ill-treat their bodies that it looks like the devil's walking parody of all four-footed things rather than the most miraculous piece of architecture, chemistry, engineering and physics in the world, a true gift of God.

The art is to find out what type of clothing suits you, helps you keep healthy and permits your body to behave naturally. Few things have been so detrimental to man's health as the myth of fashion. It is everybody's right and joy to look his best, but this does not mean the pale imitation of a popular personality wearing textiles that may restrict healthy processes.

Over fifty years back my mother's brother was living alone in North Saskatchewan, somewhere up by the Great Slave Lake. He told me several stories about the American Indians. An interesting one was that in temperatures below zero they would go about wearing just a loose, flapping shirt, and would sleep curled in a bearskin on the snow. (This was before they had all adopted the white man's ridiculous carbohydrate-rich diet.) Their skins acted as a barrier to the cold; if ours no longer do this it is an error due to living life wrongly.

When I visit my friends in Finland, sometimes the evening temperature drops to zero. We run out of a boiling hot sauna to swim in the lake; one can almost hear the body hiss. It is most stimulating and health-giving; often we just stand drinking beer and eating smoked sausage heated up on the sauna's stones. In spite of the cold and wetness after we emerge from the lake there is seldom need to do anything more than rub the hair a bit. The bodies dry themselves and nobody catches cold.

My Norwegian friends were the first to show me meshed, string underwear which permits the air to circulate beneath the outer clothing, with holes about a half inch square. It is very healthy, it is light, makes movement easy and prevents needless sweating.

The ancient Incas used to put sick people on mountaintops in sunlight and pure air to heal them. There we have it! Pure air, quite different from the smog and polluted stench that selfish industrial interests have spread over our cities.

Nevertheless, air is essential, and better polluted air than no air. Even city dwellers must try to get some air every day. A run or a swim at lunchtime, or immediately upon finishing work, will not tire you but refresh you for the rest of the evening. Do not try to do too much; better a four hundred-yard sprint than a forced mile or two. A little, regularly and often, is the best rule. And such exercise should be taken with a minimum of clothing, light shoes if running and a sensible costume for swimming. It is not advisable for people who are in poor condition to start leaving off clothing quite as drastically as I did; I was in the peak of condition at the time.

It is a good plan to get used to spending a few minutes when you get out of bed exercising in the nude, near an open window if possible except when there is a fog. But do not stand still, move! This permits the skin to absorb oxygen; few people realize how much their bodies need to take in oxygen through the skin.

Some film fans and readers of Ian Fleming's James Bond books will recall *Goldfinger,* in which a beautiful blonde is covered with gold paint and dies, starved of oxygen. People swim better in cool water rather than warm water; it permits more oxygen to reach the skin.

Human beings need air in health, and they need it even more in sickness. Many illnesses can be relieved by a change to pure air. Many sanatoria for lung complaints have been sited in pine forests or by the sea. Fever patients, on the other hand, should generally be kept away from damp, hot air. Bodington, the great reformer who insisted that tubercular patients needed pure, strong, dry air, saved more lives than any of his contemporaries who were locking patients away from air.

It is no longer questioned that air has a therapeutic value. The main problem is how much can it help? The range of conditions that benefits most by air baths is not fully understood. One recalls Gilbert and Sullivan's immortal, if ugly, Katisha:

> There is beauty in the bellow
>   of the blast,
> There is grandeur in the growling
>   of the gale.

Not so far wrong, either. If reasonably clad, but not overdressed, a stiff, energetic walk in blustery weather, striding over the 'wuthering heights,' does no harm provided one keeps walking briskly. But one should not do it on an empty stomach! A good meal with a pot of hot tea afterwards doubles the enjoyment. Hence Rupert Brooke's:

> Stands the Church clock at ten to three?
> And is there honey still for tea?

Will there ever be a poem so beautifully English as 'Grantchester'?

There should be a sincere interest in air baths, which are just as vital to health as water baths. Every air bath should finish with a brisk massage with a dry towel.

See also BREATHING THERAPY.

4

APPLE CIDER VINEGAR
AND HONEY

In 1958 a country doctor from Vermont wrote a remarkable book entitled simply *Folk Medicine*. Both in the United States and in Britain it became one of the best-selling works of the year. Dr. D. C. Jarvis was one of those conscientious figures in the world who observed truth, studied it and published the results of his researches.

He was a fifth-generation member of an old Vermont family. In brief, he was clearly convinced that the old folk medicine of the state was more effective than many of the artificial, man-made cures of allopathic medicine. As witness to this, he cited the extraordinarily large number of people who reached ages above sixty-five years, and remained actively engaged in exhaustive farming duties. The medicines which Dr. Jarvis found to be common among Vermonters were honey and apple cider vinegar.

Both his *Folk Medicine* and his *Arthritis and Folk Medicine* (1960) are full of well-detailed research and case histories which make fascinating reading. Those details considerably substantiate the remarkable claims made for both substances. Dr. Jarvis explored the acid and alkali reaction of the human body and the way in which certain foods produced either alkali or acid reactions. Probably no researcher has done so much to establish the need of the body for the mineral salt potassium, richly present in apple cider vinegar.

I would recommend that the person who is not used to its bitter taste should persevere with small doses in water, say one teaspoonful in one glass of water. When one gets used to it, apple cider vinegar becomes quite pleasant. As a first-aid medicine it is very effective indeed.

Great relief is frequently experienced when it is used for headaches, high blood pressure, severe cases of fatigue, sore throats and digestive disturbances after eating food suspected of being contaminated. Many arthritic conditions seem to react favorably to apple cider vinegar added to the diet. Small doses are usually taken in water after each meal.

Honey, taught Dr. Jarvis, is the form of sweetener which the human kidneys handle best. It has a healthy, natural laxative action, and replaces the large quantities of mineral salts, of which the body loses significant amounts every day because of natural actions such as perspiration, urination, and defecation. Dr. Jarvis was one of the first scientists to draw attention to the benefits of using natural honey instead of sugar, most of which is made from beets and not from cane, and nearly all of which is liable to chemical processes before it reaches the table of the average family.

Dr. Jarvis recorded cures of sinusitis and hay fever, using honey as the predominant therapeutic, not factory-processed honey, but the real, old-fashioned honey straight from the beehive—and there is a difference. Some manufacturers boil their honey to make it easier to get it into the jars; the boiling destroys most of the goodness in the honey! Furthermore, the doctor's researches, unique in that most allopath-trained men spend more time mocking than researching folk remedies, turned up some incomparably valuable details about the use of chewing honeycomb cappings. Kelp is also dealt with by Dr. Jarvis, and its health-giving properties are clearly set out.

No other allopath-trained doctor has ever approximated so closely to herbal and dietetic teaching as has Dr. Jarvis. His books should be bought and read by all seekers after good health.

The following quotations from *Arthritis and Folk Medicine* indicate how his findings help us.

The initial state of human tissues may well determine whether disease will find favorable soil in which to plant itself and flourish.

It is well known that the nature and characteristic of germs are modified or even completely changed with a change of environment. It is also known that the same germs may be harmless or harmful, depending on the environment and the influence that surrounds them.

Many forms of healings are linked with the patient's childhood memories and reactions to them, so that there may be some who can never stomach honey or apple cider vinegar. However, most people should try it. It is unsuitable if the patient is deficient in protein because it was originally designed to be taken after a protein meal. There seems no truth in the belief that drinking this vinegar will increase a tendency to anemia. Dr. Jarvis noted that it was long the custom of allopaths to prescribe a teaspoonful of diluted hydrochloric acid to anemic patients. Of the two, I think the vinegar is the safer.

Edgar Cayce, the famous American clairvoyant healer, would often prescribe apple cider vinegar and honey (see SPIRITUAL HEALING).

5.

AURAS

Auras are held to be of tremendous importance in diagnosis. The difficulty is that not everybody is able to see an aura, even some who have been working within the spiritualist field for many years. But then, as André Tardieu wrote: 'Difficulties lie in our habits of thought rather than in the nature of things.'

Dr. Kilner of St. Thomas' Hospital evolved what became called Kilner screens which enabled people to prove beyond doubt the existence of the human auras. We frequently see representations of saints and holy men whose heads reflect a halo or aura. These are found not only in the Christian religion, but in nearly all religious statuary regardless of the belief.

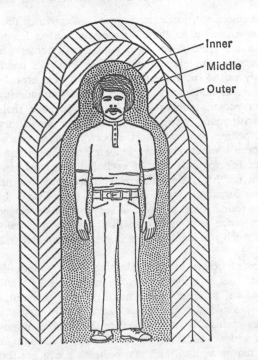

THE AURA

Clothing makes no difference to the emanation of the aura from the human body. Everybody has one; although many religious paintings show it only around the head (where it is easier to observe), it goes around the entire body. It is a light force, but unlike light in the purely materialist sense of the word.

Each aura is extremely personal, and reflects, in the colors which it shows, the character and disposition of the person. Phrenosophists call this the edge of the entity called Mind (with a capital letter this word means to them soul, intellect, etc.).

An aura comprises different layers, which on the accompanying diagram may be seen to be outermost, middle and innermost. These have different colors.

These colors are, for a clairvoyant, indicative of the health condition as well as of the nature of the person from whom emanates the aura. A sensitive person will sometimes back away from a complete stranger, refuse to shake hands with somebody unknown. Have you ever been in a crowded bus, train, plane or building, and found yourself shuddering if an unknown person touches you? This is because their aura clashes with yours; if you feel like that, it is lower than your own. Sometimes you will meet a person whom you admire, like or even instinctively love, knowing that he or she comes into your life for only a brief spell but that you can never hold him (or her). Nevertheless you treasure that meeting, and never forget the warm feeling you had. This is because you have found somebody with a very highly developed aura whose presence near your own lifts you up spiritually, and who can teach you higher things if you are able and willing to learn.

Beware of colors in your clothing; they cannot damage your aura, but wearing the wrong mixture may 'tint' your aura because it reflects your mood of the moment. Phrenosophists avoid wearing black, and usually avoid people who dress exclusively in black, since this denotes utmost materialism and an undeveloped spirituality. It is thought that wearing red or crimson and black together can predispose a person to illness.

The interesting thing about aura diagnosis is that a tendency to disease shows up in the aura long before it shows up in the body.

6.

BACH'S FLOWER REMEDIES

Strictly speaking, this is not herbal medicine in the sense that most of us know it. Dr. Edward Bach was a physician of the allopathic school who became bitterly disillusioned about the failure of allopathic medicine to heal without side effects.

He was born in 1886, entered Birmingham University at twenty, trained at University College Hospital, London, and qualified at twenty-six. He had a consulting room near Harley Street, but experience soon taught him that man-made, artificial medicines palliated rather than cured. An honest, kind and sincere man, he studied how he might best help his patients and began a profound post-graduate research project. The result of this was the establishment of certain basic principles which were influenced by Samuel Hahnemann's *Organon* (see HOMEOPATHY). Both he and Hahnemann were pathologists and bacteriologists at the London Homoeopathic Hospital from 1919 onwards.

Bach saw that the allopathic trend was to study disease and not the patient. He realized that patients required different treatment although outwardly suffering from the same illnesses, and that patients who corresponded in personality and characteristics responded to the same remedy even when suffering from different illnesses.

At this point it is only fair to interject that Culpeper's interpolation of astrology into herbalism may have been far in advance of his time, but it is the nearest orthodox herbalism came to Bach's work. The idea is found in Hippocrates' works, but as several of his books were destroyed by political or religious bigots, we can never guess how much the Father of Medicine knew.

It says much for herbal medicine that Bach excluded the large, more widely used, homeopathic pharmacopoeia and turned to non-poisonous flowers, twigs and buds for their healing virtues. In all, he narrowed his material down to thirty-eight remedies, each of which was prescribed for mental conditions without any regard for the physical symptoms. Strange though this may seem it has some support in the diligent research of the late Dr. Flanders Dunbar, one of the world's greatest authorities on psychosomatic (relating to the effect of mind on the health of the body) medicine.

In all, Bach classified human mental conditions into seven major groups, in just the same way as the latter-day

phrenologists classified human faculties—but not identically.
One group is concerned with the different types of fear, for
which would be prescribed aspen if the fear was of the unknown, red chestnut if the fear were for other people, rock
rose if it were just stark terror, or cherry plum if the person
feared losing self-control, losing life, health or sanity. Another group is concerned with doubts. I recall Kipling's line:
'Those afflicted by doubts and dismays are mightily helped by
a dead man's touch.'

Fortunately Dr. Bach's remedies were not so drastic. For
doubt in oneself he recommended Cerato, a shrubby garden
plant with blue flowers and reddish leaves and twigs. For excessive caution and hesitancy he recommended Scleranthus, a
small plant found sometimes in wheatfields. For those who
suffer discouragement easily gentian was used. I knew a Swiss
mountain guide who was an exceptionally powerful yodeler,
and nothing discouraged him at all, and he was very partial to
drinking Enzian, which is made of gentian.

There are people who suffer from advanced hopelessness,
and for them gorse was specified. It is an old tradition in England that when gorse is out of bloom, kissing is out of season.
(Thank God it is never wholly out of bloom.) When the
Swedish Father of Botany saw an entire heath ablaze with
gorse in the glory of the sunshine, he fell on his knees and
thanked God for the sight. For frustrated ambitions (some
cases of cancer have been suspected of being caused by
these) Dr. Bach found wild oats very helpful.

There is a mood which may be classified as covering de-
tachment from present surroundings. Bach would employ old
man's beard (*Clematis vitalba*) for people who were unhappy with present conditions and lived in a dream world
of castles in Spain. The cloying nostalgia for the past he
would treat with honeysuckle (*Lonicera caprifolium*). Those
who felt drained of all energy, of all mental reserves, were
treated with olives. The ancient Greeks and Romans used
olive as a medicine and source of nutrition more than almost
any other fruit.

People with various depressions were given a prescription
of mustard or white chestnut buds.

Feelings of isolation, neglect by others were dealt with with water violets, heather of Impatiens.

People unduly suffering from the influence of others would be divided into groups who could be treated with agrimony, centaury or walnut. Walnut was to strengthen people to establish their own positive personality, centaury to lift people from submission to independence. Holly would be employed against hatred, absence of love and negative emotions. Pine, larch, willow, star of Bethlehem and oak were prescribed for very severe cases of mental negativity.

Vervain was a favorite Bach remedy for those who exhaust themselves in the service of others or for a cause.

It is not widely known that the good doctor experimented widely upon himself with nearly every remedy. He devoted most of his life to the service of his researches. He joined the Great Majority at the early age of fifty in 1936.

7.

BATHS

Cleopatra, we are told, bathed in asses' milk to increase and preserve her beauty; she was one of the most beautiful women ever recorded in history. José Maria de Heredia wrote a 'perfumed sonnet'[1] about her which ends:

> *Et ses yeux n'ont pas vu, présages de son sort,*
> *Auprès d'elle, effeuillant sur l'eau*
>   *sombre des roses,*
> *Les deux enfants divins,*
>   *le Désir et la Mort.*

[1] And her eyes have not seen the harbingers of her fate
  Close behind her, strewing roses upon the sombre water,
  The two divine children, Desire and Death.
The description 'perfumed sonnet' was Anatole France's opinion of the poem.

The ancients were well aware of the way in which the body can absorb the virtues of liquids in which it is submerged.

The Greeks, Romans and many other early peoples used baths extensively. It was frowned upon by the fathers of the Church; so much nudity, they thought, caused sinfulness, so they opted for ill health and disease instead.

The Roman baths were usually the best equipped part of any city. Apart from various sorts of baths generally available in the establishment there would be a gymnasium, library and often musical concerts provided for the patrons, all highly satisfying mental and physical refreshment.

Cold baths of short duration are known to be of considerable help to various forms of sickness. They must be followed with a brisk rubdown with a rough towel to restore full circulation. In SAUNAS (*q.v.*), however, drying may not be necessary.

Hot baths should be limited to twenty minutes' soaking, and preferably finished with a few seconds' cold shower, unless you have just finished climbing mountains. I recall one occasion when a friend and I had been caught out in an appalling cloudburst on some pitiless, shelterless gray rocks, lost our way and nearly broke our necks on the Esgair Felen. After several hours of being unable to see a hand in front of us we reached the road and our car. We drove back to the cozy, cheerful lodgings, where, radiant among the polished brasses and warm rooms, our Welsh landlady greeted us with: 'Wet you are! Wet right through, did you have a lovely time? What you need is a hot bath, it's ready waiting for you!' God bless her, she saved two lives that day, although we still chuckle at her greeting now and then.

Alternating baths: this is a minor form of the sauna. One starts warm, goes into the cold tub or shower, returns to the warm and so on. Take about three times as long in the hot as in the cold water. It is very good for circulation, and tones up the skin.

Salt baths became popular in England with the advent of Martha Gunn and the bathing machine, in which our forefathers modestly took off their layers of clothing, put on copious garments and lowered themselves into the sea.

Foam baths are mainly of psychological benefit, regardless of expense.

Sitzbath: clearly a bath to sit in rather than recline in. It is generally recommended for illnesses of the lower body, and is specially designed to cover the navel to the knees of a patient.

Foot baths: Hindus are brought up to wash their feet every night before retiring to rest. For sore or tired feet, rheumatic tendencies, a chill or the sign of a cold developing, try a hot foot bath with mustard, pine or fir needles or a spoonful of eucalyptus stirred in it. Alternating hot and cold foot baths are very stimulating for the system.

Turkish baths are of doubtful medical value. My personal opinion is that the high steam content of the steam rooms is often more harmful for the lungs and respiratory system of the patient than any beneficial effect it may have.

Scrubbing baths are often used in German health resorts. The bath is about 95°F. maximum temperature. The patient is vigorously scrubbed with a stiff brush while reclining in the bath, then briskly rubbed down with a dry, warmed towel and put to bed. It is considered efficacious for people with poor circulation or for women at the change of life. The duration of such a bath should never exceed six minutes.

Headbath or inhalation: the head is covered with a large towel, and the patient leans over a bowl of boiling water to which have been added a few drops of eucalyptus, birch leaves, fir or pine needles. It is very helpful in clearing throats, congested nasal and bronchial passages. It lasts about four or five minutes; often two sessions are taken, one after the other, using freshly boiled water, etc., for each. Compared with Turkish baths, the exposure to steam and the time taken are less.

Jet baths: the body is subjected to powerful, thin jets of cold water which are hosed onto the patient in the similar direction to the lines a masseur follows. They are particularly good for toning up the muscles.

Spas

These are places where there are natural mineral-rich waters welling from the ground. Their medicinal virtues are undisputed by any branch of the healing arts. As a guide to what they offer I append some here, but the list is selective.[2]

Aachen popular for rheumatic sufferers, skin and stomach complaints.

Aix-les-Bains mainly internal disorders.

Aix-les-Thermes skin complaints, stomach disorders; once used against leprosy.

Bath gout, rheumatic and skin complaints.

Buxton gout and rheumatic ills.

Carlsbad no longer operational under the present regime, but once very popular for several complaints.

Cheltenham salt springs.

Droitwich the word *wych* meant a salt spring in Old English.

Epsom mineral salts, which are noted for clearing the bowels, etc.

Harrogate chalybeate, saline and sulphurous springs (about eighty different).

Lucca chalybeate, etc. Many uses.

Malvern Bad Salzuflen and a host more towns possess springs of mineral waters, some of which contain unique trace elements.

One allopathic medical work I consulted referred to mineral water resorts as 'going out of fashion in the light of modern medical research'. This could not be further from the truth; the difficulty is getting a booking at such a resort.

Most allopaths are satisfied with the healing properties of such waters, and many of them have lucrative practices in these resorts.

[2] Most consulates and tourist offices have information of the spas and medicinal baths available in their countries.

8

BIOCHEMISTRY

It sometimes happens that we perceive something in a blaze of light, recognizing a fact that was there for all to see. A friend of mine from overseas was a welcome guest at my home. Hardly had he been in the living room for a few minutes than he exclaimed: 'What a beautiful painting that is!' It had been nearly twenty years since that I had bought it. I had passed it every day, it pleased me certainly, but only when my friend gave vent to his feelings upon beholding it did I begin to study it seriously, in spite of having done art appreciation lectures for eighteen months when I was younger.

Dr. Wilhelm Heinrich Schüssler was one of those benefactors of the human race who drew our attention to something that is obviously true, and demonstrated how important it is for all of us. Rarely has one man worked such havoc in the field of soi-disant orthodox medicine, for until he saw the light of reason, he was himself an allopath. Discontented with the methods taught to him, and dissatisfied with the results achieved by allopathic medicine, he was driven by keen intellect and natural curiosity to the pursuit of logic and experiment.

He was exceptional because his studies did not just involve one faculty. He was a fully qualified physiological chemist and eminent physicist. He benefited from the work of Antoine Laurent Lavoisier (1743–94), a scientist murdered by political fanatics during the French Revolution, who demonstrated that burning is due to combustion with oxygen and that fire does not take place without oxygen. He was also influenced by his contemporary Justus von Liebig (1803–73), who had been made professor of chemistry at the age of twenty-one and whose contributions to organizing chemistry as a proper science gained him undying fame;

his field was the chemical and physical constitution of bodies. Schüssler also learned from Samuel Christian Friedrich Hahnemann (1755–1843), discoverer of the principles of HOMEOPATHY (*q.v.*). Schüssler followed his homeopathic methods himself.

While Schüssler was investigating this, another German, Rudolf Virchow of Schivelbein, Pomerania (1821–1902), had demonstrated that the body of man consists of minute, molecular cells, each of which has within its make-up water, as well as organic and inorganic chemical stuff. Experiments upon cremated persons showed twelve basic salts remaining as constituents of the human physical frame.

Schüssler progressed indefatigably until his researches enabled him to demonstrate that twelve salts are always found in every human being in a normal state of health. The corollary to this was that any imbalance or deficiency of those salts singly or in combination was found in every known case of ill health. With Teutonic thoroughness, the doctor proceeded to experiment and explore until he could identify distinctly and logically which salts were absent or deficient in specific illnesses.

It is incredible that the medical profession as a whole neither listened to this genius Schüssler nor examined his findings. But to present facts and logic to the established authorities is seldom as rewarding as playing Addinsell's 'Warsaw Concerto' to the stone circle of Avebury Ring.

The success of Schüssler's methods has led to the growth and popularity of what is now called biochemics. Firms all over the civilized world make and market the twelve tissue salts in homeopathic doses. Strictly speaking this is not a branch of homeopathic medicine, but it employs the simple dosages of that healing art.

One of the problems that beset the new therapist was how to administer the biochemic tissue salts. The mineral salts are difficult to handle at the best of times, but thanks to the influence of Hahnemann and Virchow, Dr. Schüssler saw that the therapeutic effect was based upon cellular constitution, and in order to render it possible for the cells to absorb the tissue salts they must be administered in extremely small, that is, homeopathic, doses, by trituration. Justus von Liebig had taught us that the smaller the particles, so correspondingly less is the resistance they meet as they encounter the tissues of the human body. What it is important to know is that the biochemic tissue salts are not administered to restore or renew the body as food or herbal drinks are given, but to renew the cells and tissues which then, of themselves, restore the natural balance. It works.

I have experimented a lot with biochemic tissue salts, and find them extremely useful as a first-aid remedy when traveling. They are light, and all one needs apart from the bottle is a watch. They must be taken every half hour, or every hour or two or four hours. Frequency and regularity are all-essential in this method of treatment. A dose consists of four or five tablets.

Some conditions require more than one salt. Then the custom is to take one lot, twenty to thirty minutes later take the second lot, and after a similar interval take the third. Leave an interval and then repeat the lots in the same order. Dr. Gilbert quoted the case of a man who, after five days of biochemic treatment, seemed and acted at least five years younger!

Here is a list of the salts with a short description of their known functions.

Calcium Fluoride (*Calc.Fluor.*) This is a constructive salt, building connective tissues, enamel on bones and teeth and fibrous elastic tissues, which enable the human body to maintain a correct degree of tensions. Its deficiency is found in cases of relaxed conditions of arteries, veins, cracks in the skin, looseness of teeth in sockets, easily decaying teeth, muscular flabbiness, varicose veins, weakness of heart (muscular especially). Extreme deficiencies have been observed in the condition called 'softening of the brain'.

Calcium Phosphate (*Calc.Phos.*) Without this, it seems no assimilation of the useful elements of foodstuffs is made satisfactorily; the nutritive particles are not properly absorbed. It has remarkable powers of restoring health to tissues that have suffered during injury or sickness, because it strengthens their power to absorb nutrition. It has been found to facilitate the building of blood vessels and to ease anemic

conditions. Healthy saliva and digestive juices are rich in
Calc.Phos.

Calcium Sulphate (Calc.Sulph.) This is found in all
healthy connective tissues; it aids normal metabolism, keeps
membranes healthy and prevents the skin diseases that are a
sure sign of its deficiency. Skin and nerve tissue are so nearly
related as to behave nearly identically, and this salt is a help
in several nervous complaints.

Nearly all eruptions on the skin and in the flesh below the
skin are aided by taking this salt. Several glandular disorders
are related to a serious lack of Calc.Sulph. Gumboils, kidney
and pancreas diseases are aided by taking it. It has the ability
to clear out decayed and toxic matter from the human system. It has preventative powers: try it if you think you've a
sore throat or catarrh developing; and it is most beneficial in
helping any condition of sepsis which has been neglected.

Ferrous Phosphate (Ferr.Phos.) This was the salt with
which I conducted my first experiments in biochemic treatment. Its efficacy has to be experienced to be believed. As it
explained in the section on DIETETICS (q.v.), iron carries oxygen through the body, and if there is not enough iron, then
there is not enough life-giving oxygen reaching the cells and
tissues all over us. See what happens to a plant in a warm dry
room where there is not enough ventilation, and imagine the
same wilting occurring in your own body cells—with deadly
effect. Polluted air contains less oxygen than the pure air
which Buddha, Jesus and Mahomet breathed long ago. Some
of it is still around—if we don't ruin that too.

Lack of iron and oxygen leads to overexpansion of the
blood vessels, loads of waste and toxins lying in the unswept
vessels (no oxygen to sweep them away), damage to the metabolism, circulation, to stomach and similar troubles. Muscles sag, pain occurs; and bleeding is hard to stop if Ferr.-
Phos. is lacking.

Potassium Chloride (Kali.Mur.) The actions of this salt
are rather complex in that it is usually used in conjunction
(alternate doses) with another salt. It revitalizes fibers which
have lost their natural function due to a serious deficiency of
another salt (or of this one). It is usually given for more advanced conditions, fevers and complicated respiratory ail-

ments. If the condition seems serious, always check to see whether *Kali.Mur.* can be used; usually it helps. Glandular swellings, measles, ulcerations and even warts, have been helped by this salt.

Potassium Phosphate (Kali.Phos.) This salt is found in all healthy people, particularly in the nervous system, spinal fluids and the brain. It is commonly found in foodstuffs, but is never known to survive the lightest cooking in any form. It is most suitable for all psychosomatic illnesses, since the body is readily upset if wrong or confusing orders are issued by the mind to the nervous network. Depressions, dyspepsia, migraine, neuralgia, neurasthenia, insomnia and almost all illnesses where nervous upsets are concurrent require *Kali.Phos.* As noted earlier (under *Calc.Sulph.*), there is a close resemblance between skin and nerve tissue, so this salt is very handy for serious skin disorders.

Potassium Sulphate (Kali.Sulph.) In a résumé such as this, it is difficult to condense the functions of the biochemic salts into short paragraphs, particularly this one, which is a very complex salt indeed. Briefly, it is used to reinforce the work of *Ferr.Phos.*, and its effect upon cells and tissues compares with that of a grease gun on a car; it enables moving parts to do so smoothly. Biochemists use it frequently for advanced conditions such as bronchitis (in conjunction with other salts), intestinal troubles of long standing, etc. It has been used with good effect to restore health and vigor to the hair: few people realize that the condition of their hair is an excellent barometer of their internal health. A Finnish friend visited me in London. 'I do not like the air of this city,' he said after a week. 'Look how it destroys the quality of my hair.' Some of us, living in cities, become too blasé to notice what is happening to our health.

Sodium Chloride (Nat.Mur.) Technically this is the salt most people have on the table at mealtimes, but the biochemic one is pure sodium chloride, without impurities or harmful additives.

All cells of the body are subject to the processes of osmosis, by which there is an exchange between the fluids within the individual cell and outside the walls of the cell. It is by osmosis that nutritional elements enter the cell. Sodium chloride is one of the most vital salts of all, for without it very serious illnesses and disorders take place. Strange as it seems, its lack is noticeable both in deficiency and excess of bodily fluids. This is because the salt is a regulator; nearly 70 per cent of the body is liquid (roughly the same proportion as sea to land), and human blood has the same proportion of salts as has natural sea water. (Consult *The Sea Around Us* by Rachel Carson.)

Constipation, heartburn, gastric illness, loss of sleep, neuralgia, dental troubles are some of the signs of a *Nat.Mur.* deficiency.

Sodium Phosphate (Nat.Phos.) This salt has the properties of a catalyst; it neutralizes acids. If it is deficient the body cannot assimilate nutrients from fats, has an increased tendency to rheumatic and arthritic conditions. Its functions are complex and widespread. It is only possible to give a sketchy outline here, because to appreciate the full range of its uses it is necessary to study biochemistry. It is used for stones in kidneys and the bladder, gout, fibrositis and for nervous complaints related to stomach conditions.

Sodium Sulphate (Nat.Sulph.) This salt is a cleanser, an eliminating agent which removes the toxic wastes that accumulate in the body for a number of reasons. Liver, intestines, glands (pancreas especially) all require *Nat.Sulph.* It is used for severe tropical (such as malaria), rheumatic and internal ailments.

Magnesium Phosphate (Mag.Phos.) Another salt whose vast range of functions in combination with other salts, taken in alternate order, covers such ailments as prostate gland disorders, sciatica, menstrual irregularities and especially ailments that have a nervous or psychosomatic origin. Certainly deficiency in this salt is found wherever there is trouble with the nervous cells and fibers, such as cramps, pains, twitchings, etc.

Silicic Oxide (Sil.) This salt has a quality of renewal, purging out poisons and waste matter; it blasts away pathological accretions which a sick organism cannot always reject. It has a powerful effect upon the health of the nervous system. Its deficiency is markedly noticeable when air- and blood-originated disorders produce symptoms with nervous side effects, for example, extreme reactions to normal temperatures of cold and heat, proneness to shivering or sweating, etc. It has been successfully employed for restoring bone damage, softening glands which have been damaged, and for severe abscesses, carbuncles, etc.

These are the twelve basic salts. But I should add that Dr. Eric F. Powell, noted in English biochemic circles and author of several authoritative books, claimed thirty further salts as trace elements in the body.

It is very interesting to see how many of the mineral salts and vitamins are present in quite simple herbs and plants that the less informed have been for many years urging us to destroy because they were weeds that took up space we could use for growing something 'more useful.'

It has long been my contention that botanic medicine is fundamentally a very highly developed form of dietetics insomuch as that it principally consists of introducing substances (internally or externally) into the body of the sick man, which herbs nourish the man rather than kill the disease. One of the great illogicalities of the self-styled 'orthodox' medicine is that it claims to kill germs and to destroy disease, but it cannot tell us how its chemicals could be so faultlessly selective as not to kill healthy, essential and helpful organisms in the body, as advertising material about them suggests. The continuing increase of diseases caused by taking of medicines to cure other diseases reveals how dangerous chemical suppressive drugs can be.

9.

BIRCHER-MÜESLI

The first person I shared a flat with was a very jovial Swiss friend, born in St. Gallen. It was not long before he had me eating *Bircher-müesli* for breakfast and sometimes for other meals.

Maximilian Oskar Bircher (1867–1939) was a Swiss physician (an allopath to begin with). He made a significant contribution both to dietetics and to natural healing.

Although he is chiefly known for his *müesli* his work was generally concerned with the values of fresh, raw, uncooked foods. He showed how up to 70 per cent of vitamins, mineral salts and nutritive elements can be lost from food by cooking it!

His traditional *müesli* mixture is made in this fashion:

3 small or 1 really big apple grated up small with the peel
1 teaspoonful of wheat germ or raw oatflakes
3 teaspoonfuls of water
1 teaspoonful of hazelnuts (or walnuts, etc.)
1 teaspoonful of pure honey
2 teaspoonfuls of raw, pure yoghurt (not processed, artificially flavored popular brands)
1 teaspoonful of raisins
The juice of half a lemon or of one orange.

NB: You can use cream instead of yoghurt, or even condensed milk.

Stir it well and eat it—what a meal! So simple to prepare, very delicious, and very nutritious.

10.

BREATHING THERAPY

This is related to the therapeutic effects of YOGA (*q.v.*), which also makes use of respiratory exercises.

It was once common for doctors with a fine sense for the more natural avenues of healing to recommend their patients to take a change of air. Psychologically it is beneficial to go away and breathe the air as once Odysseus breathed it long ago, to avoid the chemical-laden, polluted smogs which crown the overpopulated centers in which men congregate. Physiologically, the effect of good, healthy air upon the lungs and circulatory system is without equal.

Many people simply do not know how to breathe. In London there was once an organization that sold a course to teach people how to obtain therapeutic effects from breathing. Breathing rhythmically and deeply has been known to ease nervous tensions most effectively.

Breathing is normally so automatic in association with any life process that we tend to take it for granted. One of the beneficial results of physical culture, SWIMMING (q.v.), etc. is that they oblige people to breathe more effectively. The process of breathing is twofold. It is designed to carry oxygen throughout the entire organism of the body, and it is arranged to eliminate gaseous toxins as the air is expelled.

One breathing exercise is to inhale slowly while counting to ten, hold the breath for another ten counts, then expire slowly, deliberately and forcefully for ten more. (After a while most people can do that counting twenty each time.) Another exercise which tones up the nervous system especially is to breathe in short, shallow breaths very quickly through the nose, exhale orally and follow this by a slow, prolonged exhalation. Repeating this five times is quite strenuous. Long, slow, deep inhalations, tranquilly holding the breath and then expelling it forcefully and quickly, is another powerful exercise for those experimenting with breathing.

Nervous ailments, acidity in the stomach, internal troubles and some neurotic conditions are found to benefit from breathing exercises.

See AIR THERAPY.

11

CHIROPODY (PODIATRY)

by T. J. H. N. Law, F.Phys.I., M.S.M.A., A.S.Chir.

The human foot is often the most neglected part of the body. Chiropody is the healing art which specializes in the health of the feet. Each foot comprises seven tarsal bones: of these, the astragalus, which supports the leg bones, and the calcaneum, which forms the heel, are largest; then come the navicular, cuboid, internal, middle and external cuneiform. There are two phalanges for each big toe, three for each of the other toes; this gives a total of twenty-six bones.

The metatarsal (or transversal) arch is the most important arch of the foot; only the first and the fifth of the five metatarsal bones should touch the ground. There are also the inner longitudinal arch (lower) and the outer longitudinal arch (higher). The arches act as shock absorbers, giving spring and elasticity to the foot, lessening the strain of the body weight. Their condition is, therefore, closely related to the human nervous system, for if they are damaged the nervous system is conducting continuous, unnecessary shocks to the brain. If the muscular tone of the body suffers, the arches and the ligaments which support them collapse partially or wholly, and fallen arches can lead to many complications.

At birth the foot is normally balanced and able to carry the body, but ill-fitting shoes and boots bring untold troubles in their wake, deformities to their toes, depressing of the arches and many more complicated conditions. High-heeled shoes may look chic, but they can damage the feet and upset the nervous system and internal organs of the body. Taken in time, such troubles can be corrected by a chiropodist, surgically if needed.

There are other physical conditions which appear first on

the feet. Corns can be an outlet for uric acid, and acids from the body sometimes make the nails thicken, although this also occurs in some parasitic infections (for example, ringworm). It is sometimes doubted whether internal diseases do bear any relationship to conditions manifested in the feet, but gout, known to be related to the uric acid content of the blood and to the kidneys, is frequently seen there. Many stomach conditions are irritated by the condition of the feet (see FOOT ZONE THERAPY). Chilblains (related to poor circulation), callosities in general and bunions are often found in specific types of patients. There are many other discomforts of the body which disappear when they are healed by a chiropodist.

Care should be taken to wash the feet every day. People who feel very tired will experience relief if they wash their feet in cold water and briskly dry them. With regard to walking barefoot, which has come back into fashion lately, in theory it is very healthy, but the dust of man-made cities is neither as refreshing nor as comparatively clean as the earth of the countryside. So very great care must be taken to keep the feet clean and free from cuts and sores.

12.

CHIROPRACTIC

This is a scientific offshoot of the art of massage, but one which developed in a different way and with a slightly modified theory.

Daniel David Palmer of Iowa established this new science in 1895 after hearing from a man who claimed his deafness had started following a strain while working in a cramped position. Palmer examined the man, whose name was Harvey Lillard, and observed that one of his vertebrae was badly displaced. Palmer gave an instinctive, positive thrust and the bone snapped back into its proper place. He massaged the area for a week with powerful movements to keep it in place. Shortly after this, Lillard's hearing returned to him.

Palmer began a prolonged study of books on anatomy and physiology. He conducted a number of other remarkably successful adjustments which brought great relief to the patients, and he continued his researches. Problems such as backache, bursitis, constipation, heart troubles, hypertension, neuralgia and conditions of the urinary tract yielded to his healing hands.

Palmer soon established some simple facts which remain the basis of chiropractic science:

1. Impulses are properly transmitted through the nerves, and produce normal functions in a state of health.
2. Any sort of pressure upon any part of the nervous system affects the efficiency of the nervous system, exaggerating or diminishing its capacity for transmitting impulses.
3. Pressure can be caused by substances adjacent to the nerve(s), by irritation of the sensory nerves, by toxins which can irritate sensory nerves, inducing muscular contractions with a resultant pulling of the bone out of its correct position.
4. Slight pressure upon a nerve irritates; increase of irritation produces alteration of function which may develop even to a degree of paralysis.

It is significant that the development of chiropractic began in the same year in which Wilhelm Conrad von Röntgen discovered what are now called X rays; he was awarded a Nobel Prize in 1901. Chiropractors were among the first to use X rays for diagnosis, and the study of them is essential to chiropractic examination.

The layman has little idea of the vast extent of the human nervous system with its network that extends into the teeth, the ends of hair and the entire surface of the skin. Without bones, muscle or skin, the nervous system, unaided, would present a three-dimensional picture of the person's body, 'warts and all,' as Cromwell would have said.

The Nervous System

The nervous system is discernible in the embryo at a very early stage. There are three types of nerves: receptor (sensory) nerves which convey messages to the central telephone exchange (brain), motor (efferent) nerves which send out orders to the muscles, etc., and the adjustors, the intermediate neurons which coordinate the various complex commands. It is significant that man possesses more adjustor cells than any other being. The nervous system is based upon fibers and a cell unit called the neuron, which consists of a nucleated body with branching protoplasmic processes (dendrites) whose almost invisible filaments intermingle with those of the adjacent cells, and one branch longer than the rest, the axon. Impulses pass from one cell to another through these ramifications.

The nerves appear to receive their nutritive elements from the medullated sheath surrounding the axis cylinder structure of the neuron. If anything damages the neuron, the nerve may suffer considerably. If the nerve is crushed or damaged its supply of nutritive elements is endangered. Toxic substances (such as narcotic drugs) may cause intense irritation and/or cut off nutrition by inhibiting the ability of the medullated sheath to absorb it.

The Human Spine

Firstly, do not assume that a normal spine should be perfectly straight. Nothing could be further from the truth. One curve compensates for another in the curved backbone of man; the natural curves strengthen the column and make it more pliable and flexible.

The average spine is twenty-four to twenty-eight inches long. It contains four natural curves:

Cervical, backward in a concave shape.
Dorsal, forward in a convex shape.
Lumbar, backward in a concave shape.
Pelvic, forward in a convex shape (this consists of the sacral-coccygeal region).

The reason for the curves is that they constitute the most

magnificent shock-absorbing system ever conceived, and they furthermore restrict us to movements which cannot harm the delicate internal organs.

In a state of ill health, curves can become exaggerated to a point of danger. Of the thirty-three vertebrae, there are seven cervical (the thinnest and smallest in the neck), twelve dorsal (upper back), five lumbar (lower back), five sacral and four coccygeal. In some adults the sacral and coccygeal fuse stiffly together. In many adults the sacral and coccygeal bones fuse into one bone for each section; this greatly limits their spinal mobility, and is generally symptomatic of a lack of physical exercise, for which there is absolutely no substitute at all, and it cannot be considered as conducive to health. What is average is not necessarily what is normal.

Between each bone is an intervertebral disc of cartilage which further protects the spine from shocks and jars, partic-

THE PLACE OF NERVES
ON THE SPINE

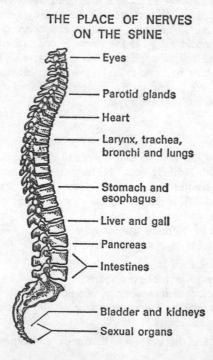

—— Eyes

—— Parotid glands

—— Heart

—— Larynx, trachea, bronchi and lungs

—— Stomach and esophagus

—— Liver and gall

—— Pancreas

—— Intestines

—— Bladder and kidneys

—— Sexual organs

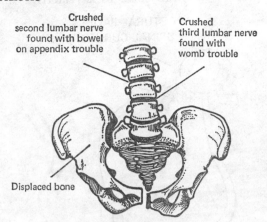

Crushed second lumbar nerve found with bowel on appendix trouble

Crushed third lumbar nerve found with womb trouble

Displaced bone

ularly softening the effect of a jolt to the nervous system encased in the spine. The health and efficiency of the discs are related to the balance of the mineral salt content of the body, and the correct proportion of vitamin intake.

Each bone has two processes joining it to the bone above, two joining it to the bone below, two transverse processes for the sides and one central spinal process. This means that the spine has a limited circumduction (how far you can twist around to one side), a rotation limited mostly to the thoracic region (chest area), very good flexion, some extension and considerable side-bending ability, especially in the regions of the neck and the lower back. For a deeper understanding of the theory and practice it is necessary to examine the importance of correct posture. Man stands upright; this places stresses upon the spine which are unknown to creatures whose spines are horizontal. A vertical spine is stronger than a horizontal spine, as the study of a column in architecture will easily demonstrate, but it has by virtue of this some inherent weaknesses which animals do not experience.

A simple examination of the diagrams will show why the health of the spinal column, and of the muscles which support it, is so important. Tummy sag, the curse of the century, affects kidneys, liver, stomach and all the internal organs, even the efficiency of the sex glands. The heavier the abdomi-

POSTURAL FAULTS
SPINAL CURVES

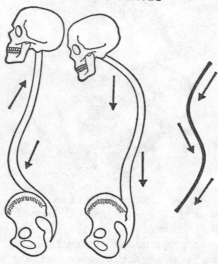

nal bulge becomes, the heavier the strain it places upon the spinal column supporting the body structure.

It will be understood that a great number of mankind's ills come from a lack of physical fitness, lack of exercise and postural faults, as Marcel Rouet expounded in his *Santé et Beauté Plastique:* 'Surely it would be better to build gymnasiums and sports places than hospitals and sanatoria?'

Chiropractic is a difficult subject to study, as it has advanced so much over the years. The researches of D. D. Palmer, B. J. Palmer (great son of a great father) and Willard Carver (the trinity who established it) have produced further successes as more details of the functions of the nervous system have come to light.

There are limitations to chiropractic which its advocates do not always detail too precisely. It cannot possibly replace mineral salts in a body which is in need of them; it cannot be a substitute for vitamins, or for physical exercise and proper dieting. But it has a great deal of logic, common sense and a long established record of success behind it.

POSTURAL FAULTS
TYPICAL STANCES

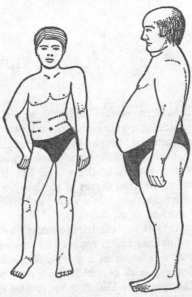

The following list gives an indication of what a trained chiropractic can treat with his manipulative adjustments: some arthritic complaints, bursitis, disc syndromes, myositis, neuralgia, postural defects, sacroiliac (lower back) pains, sciatica, shingles, spinal curvatures, sprains, strains (and associated sports injuries), also some forms of hay fever, many headaches of long standing, high blood pressure, vertigo.

The profession is well organized and has withstood the ill-informed criticisms of the allopathic doctors very well. A diagnosis invariably comprises X rays and a check on blood pressure. Also electrocardiograms and urine analysis are often carried out.

13

COLOR THERAPY

It is undeniable that certain individuals and races show marked preferences for some colors, and various shades of those colors. Primitive people prefer strong, harsh, pure colors, while delicate pastel shades are best appreciated among the most educated peoples of the world. The Sung Celadons in pale jade color, the Ting dishes of old ivory white are often so plain that the unlearned might miss the beautiful and intricate patterns worked upon them.

May I at this point explain the spectrum? This is a collection or series of images which appear as narrow bands, of one color each, within a beam of light which normally includes several wavelengths, each of which is colored; white includes all colors of the spectrum. Different sources of light emit limited wavelengths which vary considerably, and which can be analyzed with the aid of an instrument called a spectroscope. As a ray of light hits the frontier surface where two different media meet (and which are both transparent) a proportion of the ray of light is reflected back again at an angle related to the direction of the ray coming down, and the rest goes on down into the second medium where it is bent or refracted. The angle at which it is refracted is mathematically related to the angle at which it hits the second surface at the frontier. When the ray of light is refracted it is split up into its component colors of the spectrum, and each of these corresponds to a different wavelength of the light. Incandescent liquid or even solid substances also produce a spectrum, and raindrops in the air make it possible for us to perceive the rainbow or rings around the moon, as do the ice crystals found in the formation of cirro-stratus clouds (which indicate bad weather to the yachtsman if the barometer is falling).

In astronomy it has been found possible to analyze the

presence of metals and differences in surface temperatures, etc. This was mainly due to the research of a German optician, Josef Frauenhofer (1787–1826), and his fellow countryman, Robert Kirchhoff (1824–87), who developed the analysis of the spectrum and was a distinguished physicist.

The study of colors has opened up new fields in astronomy where, in Milton's phrase:

> A broad and ample road,
>   whose dust is gold,
> and pavement stars,
>   as stars to thee appear.

The purpose of the above description is to demonstrate simply that colors have more than aesthetic appeal. They have meaning and purpose, as has been demonstrated by scientists in astrophysics. What we regard as color in light waves is an attenuated form of free energy in that it relates to the atomic action within the sun (or star) from which the rays of light come.

Some very advanced modern hospitals have discovered that there are certain colors which they must not use in their decorations, or in the flower schemes, because these make patients with specific illnesses worse. For example, red and orange are found to be most difficult colors for patients in a mental ward. If then there are colors which must be avoided, it is a logical conclusion that colors may have therapeutical and helpful effects.

Let us delve further. Fortunate people who can do so journey out to the green of the countryside to refresh their nerves, calm themselves down and lose the sense of frustration which is so often concomitant with life in a busy city. Others roam out on the blue ocean in boats of various sizes, like Kenichi Horei, the twenty-three-year-old Japanese who sailed the Pacific from Osaka to San Francisco in a boat that few people would care to cross a river in, and without any electronic navigational aids. Against the blue of the sky and the gray-green of the ocean a man may enter into a world of his own, acquiring a serene mental peace. Medieval churchmen would lay sick people in the area below the colored glass windows of their cathedrals, which usually represented one saint or another; the saint was given the credit for the healing that took place.

Dr. Babbit in his *Principles of Light and Colour* outlined the results of many years of research with colors used as therapeutic agents. Although the book did not attract much attention at the time, it interested an Iranian thinker, Dr. G'hadiali, who conducted some further experiments. He cured a woman within three days of an illness that might have taken weeks to cure by other methods; his approach was to irradiate the patient with light shining through colored glass and to make sure that she drank only water irradiated with the same colors. From our study of the spectrum we perceive it may be possible that the light rays carry mineral salts which can be absorbed by the body. All that is certain is that cures have been recorded after the use of light, which today is mostly of electric source, being white light passing through specially made filters.

Most coloronic physicians proclaim the significance of mental stress and tensions behind illness, and so their approach is very close to the psychosomatic school of thought. It is not surprising that research and study has been done on this. One coloronic instrument (manufactured by Dr. Copen of Dane Hill, Sussex, England) can obtain 360 shades which can be used for the variations in human conditions.

Using only eight starter colors, it is possible to fit in a very large number of illnesses. Various shades are employed for more closely defined conditions.

Magenta: used in some heart conditions, for mental confusion, breakdown of faith and for feelings of being tied down mentally or physically.

Violet: used to ease childbirth, to stimulate the pineal gland, overcome sciatic conditions and so on.

Indigo: has been used to cure several types of deafness, help pituitary gland disorders, cataract and many other conditions.

Blue: for most skin troubles, diseases of the respiratory tract, rheumatic conditions, malaria, nervousness, anxiety, etc.

Green: related to emotional disturbances, circulatory and heart ailments, headaches and allied ills.

Yellow: liver, stomach ills, indigestion, abdominal ailments and some eye and throat diseases.

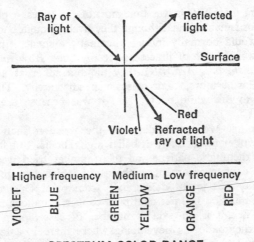

SPECTRUM-COLOR-RANGE

Orange: hernia, appendicitis, diseases of the lower abdominal area.
Red: blood and some lymphatic ailments, as well as certain nervous conditions (but by no means all).

To convey an idea of the possibilities within the coloronic healing approach I must add that the professional dyers have listed over 50,000 colors in their records.

14.

COPPER TREATMENTS

Acquaintance with African tribes in areas where copper is easily available showed up a fact which began to interest the earliest Europeans to settle in the Rhodesian hinterland. (The South was largely uninhabited when the Dutch settlers

first went there.) This was that most of the tribespeople wore
copper ornaments, and although they lived through conditions
which would normally induce rheumatic ailments (the term
covers a multitude of illnesses: see my book *How to Defeat
Rheumatism and Arthritis*) they did not suffer at all from
them. Furthermore, their wise men knew why. They explained to the white people that it was because they wore
copper.

Of course we can understand the reaction such simple
truths evoke: incredulity, disbelief and ridicule. But first one
curious rheumatic patient and then another tried wearing a
discreet copper ornament, with results which brought more
incredulity but joyful deliverance from pain. One thing is
clear: it must be 100 per cent pure copper; no alloys must be
worn. Then it is, in a large number of cases, prophylactic
against rheumatic ills developing where there is a tendency
that way, and it is in many cases curative. Basically the treatment is linked with the radiations or vibrations emitted by the
copper in the normal way.

Lieutenant Colonel A. Forbes of Sevenhampton, Glouces-
tershire, has developed some special, copper-bearing straps
which can be worn by race horses, pet animals, etc. These,
too, benefit tremendously by the copper therapy. I know a
large number of people whose work keeps them in contact
with the damp or watery conditions, and all of them have
found that wearing a ring of copper around their wrist or
ankle kept such discomforts away and helped to heal any
existing condition. It is possible to have the copper bracelets
personally polarized by radionic equipment (radiesthesia
techniques electrically applied).

15.

COUÉ'S AUTOSUGGESTION

Émile Coué (1857–1926) was born in Troyes, France, and practiced as a chemist from 1882 to 1910. On one occasion he gave a perfectly harmless bottle of medicine out (one report says it was distilled water) in mistake for another. The patient not only got better at once from the *new* medicine, but recommended it to others. Inevitably Coué realized the power of the human mind in effecting a cure by strength of will, imagination and determination. Coué was a kind, charitable, honest and sympathetic man, full of benevolence. He inaugurated a free clinic at Nancy in 1910.

He gave extensive lecture tours once he had built up his theory into a working thesis. He traveled not only widely in France but also throughout England and the United States, generally basing his theme upon the text which made him immortal in the minds of his hearers: 'Day by day, in every way I am growing better and better.'

Couéism or autosuggestion unravels one of the great mysteries of the universe. It enables a patient to get to grips with himself, to think positively and to shape his own destiny. His work recognizes the right of the personality to exist and the way in which to assert this will to live. So many people grow up in such a wholly negative way that they are mentally ill-suited and unprepared to fight disease in any form.

Of course there are limitations in view of the length and development of a diseased condition, but if people would only attend to the earliest symptoms (as I have so often said before), most serious illnesses would never take root. Sometimes people, their hearts set upon distant prospects, ignore that which is near to hand, a sort of Peer Gynt complex, or as Cowper expressed it in his poem *The Pineapple and the Bee:*

> Our dear delights are often such,
> Exposed to view, but not to touch;
> The sight our foolish heart inflames,
> We long for pineapple in frames;
> With hopeless wish one looks and lingers;
> One breaks the glass and cuts his fingers;
> But they whom Truth and Wisdom lead,
> Can gather honey from a weed.

16.

CUPPING

Once in the lonely forest lands of northern Karelia, I found a cottage by a salmon breeding farm where they showed me several cups carved out of reindeer horn. Up to fifteen of these at any one time were applied to the back, jaws, legs or neck, but never placed near the heart or the stomach.

This little-known art goes back three thousand years. The Finns brought it with them when they migrated into the marshes and swamps we now call Finland. Cuppers cure headaches, toothache, high blood pressure, abscesses, boils, etc. There are two forms of cupping: wet and dry. Near Kerimäki lives an old lady, Hilja Pylkkänen, who is considered to be a true expert in the art. She usually applies the cups in the sauna. Blood rushes up to the area as suction is created. Suction by mouth may also be used. Patients are said to feel lighter, happier and almost as if born anew. Cupping is done in the real Finnish-style sauna, which is far removed from the Western European or American misconcept called by the same name.

The profession of cupper was honored in olden days. Hilja

Pylkkänen has been practicing for over twenty years, but there are singularly few cuppers left.

This is a seemingly improbable cure, easily scorned by those who have no experience of it, but for reasons we barely understand it brings relief to sufferers. There is material for serious investigation here. An Athenian friend told me of something similar being practiced in the remoter Greek islands.

17.

DIETETICS AND VITAMINS

Allopathy and alternative healing arts approach most closely in the field of dietetics.

Natural dietetics advocate taking nutritional elements from natural sources, herbs, healthy foods and certified pure products. Allopathic dietetics allow artificial, man-made tablets and preparations containing highly concentrated vitamins. Neither school disputes the well-established scientific truths, only how they are applied. Many followers of natural healing step 'over the river' and accept pharmaceutically prepared vitamins or mineral salts, and allopaths increasingly value the therapeutic value of natural substances.

The old proverb: 'Surfeit has killed more than has hunger' might well be that of the dietetic healer who wants to teach people what to eat. There are various aspects of dietetic therapy and it is not possible to discuss all of them here.

NATURE CURE (q.v.) is basically a combination of baths, fasting and dietetics. The great apostle of nature cure is Harry Benjamin, whose writings practically established it. I deeply respect his knowledge, but some advice about fasting and citrus fruit diets may be difficult for many patients. Easier results are often obtainable from herbs.

Any person interested in healing through diet should be warned against new 'wonder' elixirs discovered and marketed by specialist health-food firms. There is seldom anything wrong with such elixirs except the price, and the fact that their virtues can often be found in dandelion, nettle, peppermint or yarrow herbal teas at a fraction of the cost.

Dietetics is very closely linked to herbal medicine, and aims to strengthen the body to make its own recovery rather than to kill the germs present during disease. We are what we eat. Our bodies reflect the type of food and drink which we absorb, excesses or deficiencies show up in complexion, digestion and, after lengthier periods of time, too often as serious illnesses.

Hippocrates seems to have been the first to apply scientific thought to the diet of man. Man has become increasingly aware that the food he consumed has a relationship to his energy and health.

More recently man has begun to distinguish between food as fodder and food as nutrition.

It is clear that health is primarily conditioned by the presence of correct nutritional elements in the daily diet. Some elements do not last longer than twenty-four hours in the body; these need replacing. We know too little of the chain links between elements and related groups as causative factors behind the colossal deficiencies which people manage to create by their eating habits, often 'digging their graves with their teeth', as someone expressed it.

The human body is the most remarkable combination of architecture, chemistry, engineering and physics in the known universe. In *Longevity and Gerontology* I referred to the work of Bogolmetz who showed that old age and death are the result of accumulated poisons absorbed from bad food, drugs, etc., clogging the delicate connective tissues between the various organs of the body, so that in effect people starve to death from lack of nutrition (although they may be overfeeding at the time!). Bjorksten claimed that we grow old because the processes of repair and maintenance in the body are hindered by the interlocking of unbroken-down molecules of protein, which has the familiar result of neutralizing nutritional intake.

Modern research increasingly refers to the intake of the body and its absorption and reaction to materials. Dietetics remove much of the mumbo-jumbo that surrounds man's concepts of health and sickness. We no longer blame evil spirits, nor can we blame germs so easily for thriving in conditions which we ourselves first create for them. As Shakespeare said, 'The fault, dear Brutus, lies not in our stars but in ourselves.'

The origin of disease lies, unpalatably enough, in man's own apathy and ignorance. Man is lazy because he is ignorant, and equally man is ignorant because he is lazy—a vicious circle. Successful living means continual, conscious effort with a clear-cut, intelligent use of time and direction of life. An unending quest for leisure and effortless existence leads to abandonment of discipline, hygiene and exercise.

'Any man with a car or a boat is obliged to spend much of his time cleaning and repairing it, in order to maintain its functions at their peak performance, to prolong its utility and its life. Few people give to their bodies as much time and care as they bestow upon mechanical appliances.'[1] Many care more about the fuel and oil they put into their cars or the boat's inboard diesel engine than they care about what they put in their own stomachs! This is a fact which brings a feeling of guilt to all of us. Most human beings eat with a carelessness that shocks the dietitian, and this is a prerequisite of disease, which is caused by the body being not clogged up with waste matter, impurities and toxins, and suffering from a lowered vitality and loss of elimination efficiency. Illness is the faulty functioning of the body as a whole. This was clearly indicated in the writings of Hippocrates and Galen but generally neglected for many centuries. 'Identical symptoms may often appear for different diseases; again, symptoms may change. . . .'[2]

The indications are that germs may well be little more than scavengers, part of whose function is to force out into the open the accumulated debris of many years of unwholesome living, unbalanced diet and uneliminated toxins.

Symptoms are the body's early warning system that some-

[1] D. Law: *Diet as a Factor in Improved Cerebral Functioning.*
[2] D. Law: *The Cause and Cure of Disease.*

thing is wrong with the whole mechanism. Hence I teach that the neglect of the smallest, slightest irregularity or any act of 'bravado' ('I'll get over that, I don't need anything') can have fatal results subsequently.

It is possible that we simply haven't finished our studies. Allow me to quote an example. Ross and other scientists established that the mosquito carries the disease of malaria, since certainly people go down with malaria when bitten by malarial mosquitoes. Is it not more likely that the injection by the mosquito destroys hitherto unidentified substances in the human bloodstream? Would it be easier, cheaper and more effective to learn what deficiency it induced than to go all over the world trying to kill off mosquitoes? From a homeopathic point of view the therapeutic to restore health might be found either in the mosquito or in some botanic substance upon which that relies.

The Importance of Mineral Salts in the Diet

Mineral salts are essential to health and to the feeling that life is worth living. They are important to build up and repair the heavy calls that life makes on us.

The first golden rule of banking is that you cannot draw out of your account more than you put in. The second rule is if you draw out everything you have in the account that account is closed. These laws also apply significantly to our health. The body has specific needs, which are expressed in daily terms, so that a need that you fail to meet one day becomes an overdraft on your health. This sort of overdraft can cause a man to fail at a critical moment and produce substandard work.

A supply of adequate and correctly balanced mineral salts retards old age, keeps you healthy and facilitates resistance to illnesses, many of which originate in a chronic lack of mineral salts in the daily diet.

In advanced dietetics we speak of osmotic equilibrium. When nutrient material comes to the lymph and the bloodstream, it is in the form of a liquid solution. The cells of the human body are, so to speak, in semiliquid form, and contain particles of dissolved matter. If the lymph which is outside these cells contains as much dissolved matter as there is within the body cells it surrounds, these cells may be dissolved or shrink. If there is more dissolved matter inside the cells than in the lymph, those cells are liable to swell dangerously, sufficiently to self-destruct. Balanced mineral salts are required to keep a healthy equilibrium.

Potassium

This is responsible for the dispatch of oxygen throughout the body. It stimulates the oxygenization of the muscles and all other tissues. Without potassium you will recognize a lack of capacity in your muscles, which will translate itself to you as 'lethargy'. Sufficient potassium enables you to make full use of natural physical energy. It also brings energy, especially to that greatest muscle of all, the heart. Potassium facilitates the expansion of the lungs and the absorption of life-giving oxygen.

Insufficiency of potassium produces a marked tendency to insomnia. If sleep eludes you, look to your diet; never take chemical sleeping pills. Often pills suppress symptoms of mineral and vitamin deficiency. I have never met an insomniac who had not marked deficiencies of mineral salts and vitamins, even where the insomnia was of psychosomatic origin. A lack of potassium means that injuries heal slowly. Pain is more acutely felt when potassium is absent. There is a distinct connection between a diet deficient in potassium and many forms of baldness.[3]

Most forms of bacteria are dependent upon moisture and they need to absorb moisture from the body, but if there is a high potassium content in the cells, the bacteria are destroyed, for it dries moisture out of them.

There are many foods rich in potassium, but cooking destroys much of it before it ever gets to our stomachs. Carrots, kohlrabi, onions, parsnips, spinach and turnips lose at least 70 per cent of their potassium when they are cooked. Asparagus, cabbage, cauliflower, corn, nuts, oats, string beans and tomatoes lose between 50 per cent and 60 per cent when they are

[3] See *How to Keep Your Hair On*, by Donald Law.

cooked. Baked kippers and steamed cod are rich in potassium. So are blackberries, coconut, cranberries, endive, figs (dried), grapes, honey, lettuce, marrow, molasses, nuts, oats, olives, paprika and watercress.

There are many rich herbal sources of potassium, such as herbal teas. Carrageen, dandelion leaves (excellent in salads), fennel, mint, mullein, parsley, peppermint, primrose flowers, summer savory and yarrow are well known to herbalists for their potassium content. (See APPLE CIDER VINEGAR.)

Potassium and salt exist in a continual state of war. Sodium (ordinary table salt) when taken in large quantities draws not only fluid out of the cells of the body but robs them of potassium as well. It keeps the extracted fluid floating around the tissue, so much so that about a teaspoonful of salt will retain about a pint of superfluous liquid in the body. Dieters, instead of taking chemical pills, should leave ordinary table salt alone and increase their potassium intake.

Another source of potassium, which comes straight to us from the 'Whales' path' as the Anglo-Saxon epic poem *Beowulf* calls the sea, is the remarkable deep seaweed we call kelp. Dietitians investigating the traditional diet of Japan discovered that, far from being exhausted by the large bulk of carbohydrate foods they ate, the coast dwellers of Japan were quite healthy. This is because of the large amount of seaweed foods eaten. In Norfolk the sea plant called samphire (*Crithmum maritimum*) is still commonly eaten; it is very tasty and extremely nutritious, despite its appearance. Kelp (*Macrocystis pyrifera*) and other seaweeds, including bladder wrack (*Fucus vesiculosus*), all loosely known as kelp (the word comes from the Middle English *culp* meaning any tangle or wrack), are the usual components of 'seaweed' tablets or deep sea mineral salts which are on sale. Such tablets are easier to take and often tastier than raw preparations. They are rich in nutrient substances.

About one third of the content of sea plants is health-giving mineral salt. Potassium is one of the main ingredients, but fifteen other mineral salts can be found in kelp, also essential vitamins as well, such as A, B, E, etc.

Phosphorus

This salt is intimately concerned with the life and the structure of body cells.

Deficiency of phosphorus goes with deterioration of the bones, thus producing an accident-prone liability to fracture. Phosphorus deficiency is usually followed by a deterioration of the health of the lungs also. Some leading authorities think even tuberculosis can develop. 'Because there is a significant connection between phosphorus in the diet and the efficiency of the nervous system, lack of this mineral salt induces a loss of virility, loss of stamina, twitching muscles, an inefficient correlation of action between brain and muscles.'[4] It gives quick responses expressed in muscular action, and an alert, healthy, efficient, quick-acting nervous system.

Without phosphorus there is no adequate or efficient growth of and repair of the muscles. We know that muscular exertion produces conditions within the muscles which require nutritive elements to repair the 'running-down', and these repairs demand phosphorus in the diet. Experiments show that sufficient phosphorus is essential if muscular contraction is to be complete; half-contractions get you nowhere.

Phosphorus enables the glands to secrete their vital fluids correctly in proper proportions. It neutralizes excessive acidity and makes it possible to effect the correct metabolism of fats and starches. The action of lecithin, the fat-dissolving agent, is aided by phosphorus. An absence of red blood cells in the body may well be due to a deficiency of phosphorus which is required for their manufacture. Recent research has confirmed that the cells of the brain contain about 100 mg phosphorus per ounce of brain. But you will not become 'brainier' by eating large amounts of it!

There is, however, a limit to the amount of phosphorus that a human being can absorb. There must at all times be a ratio of 1 part calcium to every 1½ parts of phosphorus. In order to keep this ratio in correct proportion, two things are needed: a regular supply of vitamin D and most espe-

[4] D. Law: *Diet as a Factor in Improved Cerebral Functioning.*

cially pure honey. Should the ratio of phosphorus to calcium rise to as much as 6 parts to 1 part, rickets develops. The Danish proverb says: 'Enough is great wealth.' I commend it where diet is concerned.

There is one caution I must give to those who eat a heavy meat diet. Meat is almost invariably very rich in calcium, another mineral salt. If you eat a lot of meat you need correspondingly more phosphorus; and thus more vitamin D must be consumed.

Phosphorus-rich foods are barley, brown rice, cabbage, cheese, eggs, fruit (generally), halibut, kidneys, lentils, liver, milk (and milk products), nuts (especially almonds, hazelnuts, peanuts and walnuts), oats (particularly coarse-grained natural oats), okra pods, oysters, peas, peanut butter, radishes, salmon, sardines, sesame, shrimps, watercress and wheat germ. There are some excellent herbal sources of phosphorus, among which are calamus, caraway seeds, chickweed, garlic, licorice root, marigold and meadowsweet flowers and sorrel.

There is one point I should emphasize. Insist upon having eggs that come from free-range hens. A hen that runs about in the open air and sunlight, scratching up natural minerals from the soil, lays a more wholesome, nutritious egg than a poor creature that spends all its life in a prison cage, never seeing natural sunlight (for which ultraviolet rays are no substitute), eating no natural food, consuming only chemicals. Considering what some people eat there is little wonder at the poor standard of health preponderating in civilized countries today where kidney diseases, cancer and the like flourish as never before in human history.

Iron and Copper

Iron will only function properly in the human body when an adequate supply of copper is present. Lots of sufferers from anemia say that they have tried taking lots of iron tablets, they just do no good at all. Firstly, iron is best absorbed from purely natural sources. Secondly, upon increasing copper intake a body holds iron long enough to make use of it.

Iron gives strength to the nerves and the muscles. Iron purifies the blood and makes it rich; it stimulates the production of life force and strengthens the functions of the cerebellum; it is an absolutely irreplaceable substance for the transportation of oxygen throughout the body. People who lack iron always complain of not being able to breathe properly; in short, their bodies are being starved of life-giving oxygen. Other signs of shortage of iron are: the skin goes flabby; the muscle tone sags; wounds and cuts take a long time to heal up; and there is a continuous feeling of being cold.

Iron is stored in the liver, and it has some effect upon the storage capacity of both the kidneys and the pancreas gland. Furthermore there seems little doubt that the glands benefit from a regular intake of iron. The body will only absorb iron when it is needed, otherwise it is eliminated. It is absorbed through the mucosal cells of the small intestine. The correct iron intake is related to the regularity of the heart beat. Sportsmen need about fifteen mg of iron daily when in full training. All adults need at least twelve mg daily. Half a cupful of parsley contains more iron than a quarter of a pound of liver.

Anybody who likes shooting, archery or any sport where excellent vision is required should remember that if his vision does not seem to be up to par he should definitely increase his iron intake for two weeks before rushing round to consult an oculist. Lack of iron is a sure cause of many simple forms of dimness of vision. However, it is obviously not the only cause, so try adding iron to the diet first. If the dimness persists, consult an oculist or try one of the 'better sight without glasses' courses.

The principal sources of iron are asparagus, barley, blackberries, black molasses, bran, dates, dried fruit, eggs, dried figs, lentils, lettuce, oats, olives, prunes, radishes, raspberries, rye, walnuts, watercress and wheat germ.

There are rich sources of iron in the herbs which grow happily and naturally throughout the countryside (provided man doesn't destroy the 'weeds' with chemical sprays). Emerson once remarked that 'A weed is a plant whose virtues we have not yet discovered.' Here are some: burdock root, devil's bit, *hydrocotyle asiatica*, meadowsweet, mullein leaves, parsley, rest harrow, silverweed, stinging nettles (one of the richest and best sources of iron—never destroy them, they could one day save your health), strawberry leaves and yellow dock.

One sure sign of lack of copper is graying hair! Wheat germ and black molasses are rich sources of copper, as are almonds, calves' liver, dried figs, loganberries and most nuts. I personally recommend you to use the purer and safer forms of copper found in fruit, nuts and herbs. Some reasons are given in Elspeth Huxley's book *Brave New Victuals*. Botanic sources of copper are burdock root, devil's bit, meadowsweet, parsley, silverweed, stinging nettles, watercress and yellow dock. Wheat germ contains about 0.35 mg copper per ounce.

Calcium

This is an essential ingredient of all growth and it is of inestimable value to speed recovery from illness. It is one of the chief components of the bones of the body. It gives tone to the muscles. People often learn most about it when suffering from its deficiency, as is true of many of the mineral salts.

Calcium is stored in the trabeculae of the bones, and since the whole body's needs take precedence over the welfare of any particular part, when the over-all needs of the body demand calcium, the chemical system of the body draws out supplies of calcium from the trabeculae, usually drawing it from the vertebrae first, then from the pelvis. The effects of this drawing upon reserves induces brittle, easily breakable bones and rickets (deformation of the bones). Up to 98 per cent of the body's store of calcium is deposited in the bones (including our teeth), and the remainder is in general circulation around the tissues in body fluids to facilitate the clotting of blood, maintaining easy passage through cell and tissue walls, and keeping the enzymatic action in good working order.

An early sign of shortage of calcium is a lack of sleep. People who tire easily usually lack calcium. Sometimes quite young people have complained to me of 'rheumatic pains' in their joints; often this is 'pseudo-rheumatism', caused by the draining of calcium from the bones. Sufferers from arthritis, fibrositis or rheumatism in any form will find helpful advice in *How to Defeat Rheumatism and Arthritis*.

The parathyroid gland controls the amount of calcium entering the blood. If this gland is damaged or diseased there is a dangerous fall in the amount of calcium in the blood. Diarrhea, dysentery and the like hinder the absorption of calcium from the blood. *One of the dangerous sides of kidney disease is that it hinders the storing of calcium.* The result of excessive consumption of fats is their accumulation in the body; this also lessens the ability to take up calcium.

People who suffer from a shortage of calcium should most consciously reject from their diet chocolate, cocoa and products made from these foods, and also foods which contain oxalic acid, such as rhubarb and spinach.

Under the heading of phosphorus I have given reasons why the ratio of 1 part of calcium to 1½ parts of phosphorus must be maintained.

Foods rich in calcium are almonds, apricots, beans, bran, buttermilk, cabbage, cauliflower, cheese (not processed), carrots, eggs, endive, figs (including dried figs), gooseberries, grapes, hazelnuts, herring, kale, lemons, lettuce, limes, maple sugar, milk (and dried skimmed milk), black molasses, onions, oranges, sardines, sour milk, soya beans, turnip tops, watercress and yoghurt.

There are many wonderful herbal sources of calcium. The general rule is that the darker the leaf the more calcium it contains. Sadly, people tend to throw away all the outer leaves of plants and to use only the lighter green, inner leaves —a mistake! Here are some examples: arrowroot, carrageen moss, camomile, chives, cleavers, coltsfoot, dandelion leaves (in salads), dandelion root (in substitute coffee), flaxseed, horsetail grass, meadowsweet, mistletoe, nettle, okra pods (very popular in Greek and Balkan cooking), pimpernel, plantain, rest harrow, shepherd's purse, silverweed, sorrel (also contains some oxalic acid) and toadflax. Note that the calcium content of all plants is lowered by the use of artificial fertilizers.

If you lack calcium you cannot absorb enough vitamin C. There is more nutriment, and calcium specifically, in goat's milk than in cow's milk. Techniques of pasteurization destroy a great part of milk's natural calcium content. Milk and all calcium foods are best eaten alone. If you take them at the same time as carbohydrate foods (particularly starch) you will lose half your calcium intake to start with, because the calcium simply combines with starch to form solids which go to waste and are not absorbed in the bloodstream and lymph. Generally speaking, the human body needs to take into circulation one whole gram of calcium per day. If possible this should be from natural sources.

All who suffer from a build-up of tension and nervous conditions, particularly when actually performing in public or partaking in a competitive sport, may find their nervousness greatly eased by increasing their calcium diet, or alternatively by decreasing the quantity of saturated fatty acids in their diet (found in animal fats particularly), which lessen the ability of the body to absorb calcium.

Fluorine and Fluoride

Fluorine is found in the bones and in the teeth. It is far removed from the substance of fluoride, which some ill-informed people insist upon adding to water. Natural fluorine is found in garlic and in watercress. It is a trace element, and little of it is required, so that a reasonable intake of green vegetables, particularly of watercress, suffices.

Fluoride is usually extracted from aluminum waste. At least a dozen Nobel prize-winning chemists and physicists have condemned the addition of this substance to drinking water. The concept that the addition of fluoride (sodium fluoride) to water is necessary to preserve health is either deliberate fiction or ignorance. The health of teeth nowadays is generally poor because children are given far too many sweets to eat, bribed with sweets, generally speaking, whose nutritive value is nil. The cravings of the children are genuine enough, but they are quite unable to tell their parents that what they need are mineral salts. Instead of sweets, chocolate and ice creams, parents ought to give their children (and themselves) such foods as sesame seeds, sunflower seeds, honey, dried bananas (a very fine treat), apples and other fruit in season.

Because of the commonly faulty, mineral-deficient diet of the majority of women before pregnancy, fetuses are developed in bodies with marked mineral deficiencies. (British children are especially short of calcium and silicon.)

The duty of all thinking men and women is to protest and complain to the authorities with monotonous and forceful regularity until the practice of fluoridation of water supplies is discontinued. There was a report in the Paris *Aurore* (July 13, 1967) of the Fourteenth Congress of Dentists, where over ten thousand dental surgeons from all over the world refused to sanction the use of fluoride, and categorically stated that there was insufficient evidence that it could protect the teeth from decay.

Manganese

This controls the rate of release of energy from foodstuffs and their rate of being used by the body. It is known to be essential to the healthy functioning of the pituitary gland. Manganese is antiseptic and a natural tonic to the nervous system. It keeps the linings of bodily organs in a healthy state.

It is found in agar-agar, almonds, raw egg yolk, endive, liver, mint, nasturtium blooms, unsalted olives, parsley, peanuts, peppermint (the herb), potatoes, walnuts and wheat germ.

Silicon

This gives hardness to bones and teeth. It is essential for maintaining the alkaline balance of tissues and it facilitates quick nervous reactions. It contributes to healthy eyesight. Older people who are worried about their eyesight often suffer from a shortage of silicon in their diet. It is said that the eyes contain about twenty times more silicon than do the muscles. Silicon increases the capacity to work hard and steps up energy output. There is about 20 per cent less silicon in the skin of older people than that found in young people.

Many listless, 'stale' days in a gymnasium or on the sportsfield owe their origin to a deficiency of silicon. Deficiency also results in speedy exhaustion, nervous debility, irritability due to physical conditions and a tendency to suffer from cold feet and hands and early loss of hair. There is generally a silicon deficiency in cases of obesity and rheumatism. (I know of several cases where a deficiency of silicon was diagnosed by doctors as a deficiency of calcium.)

Silicon is found in horsetail grass, comfrey, dandelions, herbnettle, houndstongue and lungwort. Foods containing silicon include artichokes, asparagus, barley, cabbage, celery, cucumber, leeks, lettuce, liver, milk, mushrooms, nuts, oats, spinach, strawberries, sunflower seeds, tomatoes and turnips.

Iodine

The scavenger cells of our bodies (phagocytes) need iodine to do their marvelous job efficiently. Hence there is a connection between our iodine intake and the capacity of the body to resist disease and keep up the radiant, glowing good health which is the hallmark of every sportsman. Iodine enables us to use the brain cells and the nervous system at our disposal to the very best of our ability. A good supply makes for calm thinking, coolheadedness, logical appreciation of taking risks such as in ski jumping, diving, mountaineering, etc. The thyroid gland needs a regular supply of natural iodine for its healthy functioning. Iodine is an oxidizing catalyst; it burns up the food intake and prevents the formation of fat. But do not start taking large quantities of it if you are very overweight; an excess of iodine is powerfully toxic! Iodine enables muscular tissues to store oxygen, and gives better muscular efficiency and staying power.

Chlorine facilitates the loss of iodine from the body, so that the more chlorine you absorb the heavier the loss of iodine is likely to become. This warning applies not only to those who swim, dive and play water polo, but also to anybody who drinks water which is treated with chlorine before it comes out of the tap.

Foodstuffs containing iodine are: agar-agar, artichokes, asparagus, bananas, carrots, egg yolk, garlic, leeks, lettuce, melons, mushrooms, mussels, onions, peas, rhubarb, spinach, strawberries, watercress.

The herbal sources of iodine include: bladder wrack

(*Fucus vesiculosus*), dulse, Icelandic moss, Irish moss and garlic. Throughout America the *Macrocystis pyrifera* is more frequently used than the *Fucus vesiculosus* form of kelp, but their chemical analysis of mineral salts, etc., is almost identical from the point of view of nutrition.

Zinc

This contributes greatly to the efficiency of muscular control by the mind. It facilitates the coordination of mind and muscle. It aids the metabolism of both proteins and carbohydrates, thus creating energy. It is of value in controlling the storage of both sugars and starches. It aids the respiration of the tissues.

Without zinc there seems to be a decreased efficiency in the manufacture of male hormones, leading to a weakness in the reproductive organs. It is a little sad and a little painful to read some of the nonsense written by certain psychiatrists about patients whose symptoms indicate clearly—to a dietitian at any rate—that there is a deficiency of zinc and nothing fundamentally wrong at all with the patients' minds. Cases of diabetes have also been related to zinc on account of its effect upon the storage of sugar. Constipation over long periods often indicates a shortage of zinc.

We find zinc in beans, egg yolk, most legumes, most nuts, peas, vegetables' green leaves and above all in wheat germ. Since zinc is found in most green leaves it is found in many herbs.

Sulphur

Sulphur is a mineral salt with many varying functions. It is essential for a glowing healthy complexion and for sound digestion. It is conspicuous in its role of helper in the metabolism of proteins. It enables the liver to take up other mineral salts into the blood and lymph through which they are conveyed to any part of the body needing nutrition. It facilitates the healthy operation of the brain and the nervous system, but it is oxygen-consuming, so that too much sulphur may rob the body of much-needed oxygen.

I must mention here that natural sulphur has nothing to do with the present fad for 'Sulphonamide' drugs which have been on record of causing such side effects as rashes, kidney diseases, sterility, permanent heart damage, nervous disorders (even insanity) and death. Natural sulphur gives a fine, healthy sheen to the hair. It prevents constipation, wards off bronchial and respiratory ills. Agility, which is related to good eyesight, is connected with the sulphur intake. Sulphur is naturally present in human blood, but needs to be regularly taken in.

Sources of sulphur are almonds, brussels sprouts, cabbage, cauliflower, coconuts, cottage cheese, chestnuts, cranberries, cucumber, red currants, egg yolk, figs, garlic, horseradish, black molasses, okra pods, onions, oranges (grown naturally without any chemical sprays), potatoes (most nutritious when baked in their jackets in a slow oven), pineapple, radishes and watercress.

There are a large number of herbs which contain sulphur in rich quantities. Among these are broom tops, calamus, carrageen, coltsfoot, eyebright, fennelseed, meadowsweet, mullein, pimpernel, plantain, rest harrow, shepherd's purse, silverweed, stinging nettles and waywort.

Magnesium

This has a part in the composition of our bones and teeth. It is a catalyst which helps absorb the carbohydrates which form a large part of the average diet. It is a remarkably powerful acid which eliminates food wastage from our bodies. We know that the adrenal glands will not function properly without magnesium.

Deficiency of magnesium is rare, but when it does occur it causes obstinate constipation which is not curable by simple medication. It also brings nervousness and sleeplessness, and makes people feel cold and heat with exceptional sensitivity. Deficiency of magnesium also induces an unhealthy acid condition of the blood, particularly in people who eat a lot of sugar. A very rapid and urgent substitution of honey for sugar intake is advisable because magnesium is present in honey. I have also encountered magnesium deficiency among some of the *pieds-noirs* of what used to be French North and West Africa: this may be a local deficiency. Large doses of magnesium, on the other hand, act as a depressant agent on the human nervous system, and should be avoided by healthy people.

Traces of magnesium are found in a large range of food-stuffs. Good quantities are also found in citrus fruits, egg yolk, figs, oats, prunes, spinach, dairy foods (natural and not processed), legumes, nuts (especially almonds and coconuts), watercress and pure untreated whole-grain foods together with honey and kelp.

Magnesium-rich plants are bladder wrack, black willow (bark), broom tops, carrot leaves, devil's bit, dulse, dandelion (herb), *Hydrocotyle asiatica,* kale, kelp, meadowsweet, mistletoe, mullein (leaves), okra, parsley, peppermint, primrose, rest harrow, silverweed, skunk cabbage, toadflax, walnut leaves and wintergreen.

Sodium

Sodium is a component of the body. (Salt is sodium chloride.) All the fluids of the body contain traces of natural sodium, and specifically the gastric juices. Its primary function is to help rid the body of acids. By the same token it prevents the other constituent mineral salts in the body silting up the bloodstream. This means that quick muscular contraction depends largely upon the amount of natural sodium in the blood. Sodium is an agent in the speed of coagulation of the blood.

A great deal of sodium is lost by perspiration during strenuous activity, exercise, etc. Now, whereas some sodium is lost in urination, this loss is generally controlled by the kidneys. When it is lost in the form of sweat, the body has no mechanism with which to hold back the mineral salt content. The solution to this is to take foods or tablets containing mineral salts after exercise (and after sauna or Turkish baths).

Sodium deficiency causes some cases of cramp. All scratches, wounds, etc., are slower to heal if there is a sodium deficiency. Unfortunately many people try to overcome this deficiency by eating sodium chloride (table salt), each gram of which can retain up to seventy grams of liquid in the body. Thus a spoonful of salt can keep about a quart of totally unnecessary liquids in the body. People noted for their high rate of salt consumption become stout from about thirty onwards. Germany, where more salted meat is eaten than in the rest of Europe, has one of the highest rates of death from heart diseases. In Denmark and Iceland, both countries with a very high rate of consumption of salt fish, there are alarmingly high rates of death from cancer. Tumors contain more fluid in their tissue than any other known form of tissue. Salt keeps fluid in the body, so the result is not unexpected.

Table salt contains less magnesium and potassium than does sea salt. Fortunately there are some balanced salts on the market which are non-toxic and in which the potassium and other minerals have been matched up with quantities found naturally in the human body.

Carrots, celery, Cheddar cheese, herrings (raw), lentils, nuts, oats, spinach and steak (raw) contain natural sodium.

Herbs rich in sodium are: beets, black willow, carrageen moss, chives, cleavers, devil's bit, fennelseed, meadowsweet, mistletoe, nettles, rest harrow, shepherd's purse, sorrel, watercress and waywort.

Chlorine

The mineral chlorine acts very closely with sodium. Deficiency is not common, but when it occurs it can upset digestion, cause the loss of teeth and hair, and bring about a reduction in muscular power. Nearly all plants contain rich supplies of chlorine. In large amounts it burns up too much vitamin E, reduces the iodine content of the body, accumulates fat and diminishes stamina. Butter, cheese, figs, kelp, milk, olives and radishes are rich in chlorine. All green foods contain some chlorine.

VITAMINS

Vitamin C

This vitamin is a must for those who eat a protein-rich diet. The more protein you eat the more vitamin C your body requires. It is not toxic in large natural doses. The average person needs about 400 mg daily. The British recommended intake of vitamin C is about half that recommended in the United States.

It is essential for smokers to increase their intake because each cigarette burns up about twenty-five mg! If you have a deficiency of calcium the vitamin C will not be properly absorbed. (I have listed elsewhere a number of foods which contain calcium.)

Jacques Cartier (1491–1557), the famous French explorer born at St. Mâlo, who opened up Newfoundland and Canada, was the first to connect skin disease (and scurvy in particular) with the absence of fresh fruit and vegetables in the diet. The discovery was made during his voyage of 1534. In 1795 the British Navy ordered sailors to take rations of lime juice, hence the name 'Limeys' which the Americans applied to them, and eventually to all English people.

Vitamin C is found in blackcurrants, broccoli, cabbage, cantaloupe, carrots, cauliflower, citrus fruits of all kinds (particularly guavas, lemons and limes), kale, mustard-and-cress, paprika (green is best), red chilies, rose hips (the Norwegian variety seem to be richest), strawberries, turnip tops and watercress. This vitamin is all too readily destroyed by cooking.

A marked lack of vitamin C leads to easily bruised muscles and similar internal injuries. I have long suspected a connection with hemophilia. Many hemophiliacs (who, after only a slight bruise, may easily bleed to death) seem to exhibit symptoms of chronic vitamin C deficiency. Lack of this vitamin allows bones to become brittle and to snap easily. The teeth and the gums suffer most markedly. The skin tends to look 'dead', and since the skin and the nervous system are, to

all intents and purposes, the same type of tissue, the whole
effectiveness of the nervous system tends to be well below
par. There is inertia, laziness, tiredness that cannot be explained otherwise. Stiffness is frequently due to vitamin C
deficiency.

Vitamin C accelerates the consuming of alcohol and fats by
the body, hindering the storage of fat in body tissues. It is a
good first aid for a suspected cold; take 100 mg of vitamin C
every hour for twenty-four hours.

Vitamin B

The letter B represents a large family of vitamins. There
are some twenty-four members of this group, including vitamins G (now called B^2) and H (now known as Biotin).
Energy, healthy heart action, strong nervous reflexes and
many other advantages all accrue from the daily intake of the
vitamin B complex.

B^1 is particularly useful and beneficial to the appetite and
acts as a guardian for the nervous system.

B^2 (under which heading Riboflavin, Niacin and folic
acid are all classified) is required for the healthy growth and
condition of the skin, for efficiency of eyesight and formation
of the blood. It acts as an oxygen-transporting vehicle, particularly for the carbohydrates. Many young women starve
themselves of carbohydrates when what they require to keep
fit is a higher intake of vitamin B^2.

B^3 is also referred to as pantothenic acid. It is significantly
related to the metabolism of carbohydrates, and is known to
play an important role in stiffening resistance to infections.
Insomnia, irritability and 'nerves' on the track or in the gym
are often due to lack of B^3.

B^6 Pyridoxin, as this is called, forms an essential ingredient
of neural and dermatic well-being.

Generally speaking, if you deliberately include black molasses, wheat germ, yeast and yoghurt in your daily diet you
should be very well supplied with all the vitamin B family. B^1
is found in the following foods: barley, dried beans, millet,
oats, roes (especially cod roes) and yoghurt. Large supplies
of B^2 are contained in beef, cheese, eggs, leeks, liver, Mar-

mite, milk, potatoes, tomatoes, turnips, fresh green vegetables. B^3 is found in black molasses, egg yolks, kidneys, liver, dried milk, nuts, roes (especially cod roes), tomatoes, wheat germ. B^4 (Arginine), also a useful member of the family, is found in eggs, milk, oatmeal, peanuts and yeast.

Alcohol is lethal to vitamin B in the body. A heavy drinking session may seriously rob you of energy. Penicillin seems to be a destroyer of Niacin (B^2).

I dislike stating emphatically that every human body needs specified quantities of this or that substance, but these quantities are the accepted, average, daily minimum amounts: B^1, one mg; B^2 (Riboflavin), three mg; B^2 (Niacin), fifteen mg.

Vitamin A

The 9th Cancer Symposium in Tokyo heard significant evidence that cancer is frequently found in persons starved of vitamin A. Some animals have been given cancer and then injected with massive doses of vitamin A which prevented any further development of the disease in an overwhelming number of cases.

We do know that the absence of vitamin A distinctly contributes to the slowing down of reactions. For anybody who follows one of the Japanese arts such as aikido, judo, kendo or the European fencing, a high intake of vitamin A is a must. Vitamin A was isolated in 1913 by a Yale scientist, who found it in butterfat.

Night blindness, dry or scaly skin, and easily catching colds, are symptomatic of vitamin A deficiency. Vitamin A is soluble in fats. We cannot store it; we need some every day. This is one of the most commonly encountered deficiencies. Vitamin A is measured in International Units (IU). Halibut liver oil contains 30,000 IU per gram, cod liver oil, 1,000 IU per gram; ox liver, 150 IU per gram; watercress, 50 IU per gram; dried apricots, 50 IU per gram; carrots, 40 IU per gram; butter and margarine, about 30 IU per gram. The average person needs about 5,000 IU per day.

The following foods also contain vitamin A: broccoli, cream cheese, dandelion leaves, egg yolk, kale, kidneys, lettuce, liver, milk (in Denmark milk is always bottled in dark glass to prevent the vitamins being weakened by light), potatoes, peaches, prunes, tomatoes, turnip tops.

Vitamin D

This facilitates the healthy action of the heart. It cooperates with phosphorus to burn sugar. It provides stability for our nervous system; it is vital in order to make the best use of the intake of calcium and phosphorus.

One peculiarity about vitamin D is that it is easily destroyed by alkali soaps. Thus those who take frequent shower-baths, such as divers, swimmers, football players, water-polo players, etc., must be careful to avoid alkali soaps and use herbal soaps and shampoos.

Tooth decay, bone deformation, weakness of the muscular system (weightlifters please note), rickets and other ills follow a deficiency of vitamin D. Elderly people who experience decalcification and thinning of the bones are usually victims of an accumulated deficiency of vitamin D.

Sportsmen need about 2,000 IU daily. Vitamin D is found in butter, cheese, kidneys, liver oils (cod and halibut), mackerel, margarine, salmon, sardines and tuna. It can be absorbed from sunlight but as soon as you become tanned the body stops absorbing it!

Vitamin E

This vitamin is commonly supposed to be the 'fertility' vitamin. Here I must examine some misconceptions about the mystique of fertility. Man has tended to be baffled by the problems involved in his own sexuality. When he does not want to be fertile he finds he is, and when he desperately requires to reproduce his own kind he often cannot. Such things can never depend upon man alone; there are other factors involved. Fertility depends upon the health of both partners and certainly not on taking large doses of any one particular vitamin. While it is fairly certain that without vitamin E the fertility rate will fall, it does not follow, conversely, that with it fertility is inevitably going to rise.

Persons unaccustomed to a high vitamin E intake who start

a marked increase could experience a rise in blood pressure which is undesirable.

The blessings which a supply of vitamin E bestow upon us are energy, the shielding of vitamins A and C (without E the essential vitamins A and C are lost), a healthy heart and good circulation. Diabetes has been known to respond to doses of vitamin E. A few cases of muscular dystrophy in the United States have been recorded as having been cured after vitamin E treatment.

Muscles need vitamin E to keep their tone. It also lessens the chances of having a stroke. It is an anticoagulant, so that no hemophiliac should take large doses. It is a vitamin which is fat soluble, so that fried foods destroy it. Mineral oils, chlorine, many animal fats, some medicines that contain ferric chloride or similar salts may damage your natural store of this vitamin. The use of steel rolling mills instead of quorn-stones has been found to destroy vitamin E, so that the 'white' flour and bread on sale are generally lacking in all the natural goodness of the wheat germ.

Brown rice, eggs, lettuce, sunflower seeds, watercress and wheat germ are some of the best sources of vitamin E. Corn oil, cotton oil, peanut oil, soybean oil, sunflower seed oil and, of course, wheat germ oil are all easily obtainable, particularly the last, and all are rich in vitamin E. I recommend peanuts and wheat germ as the basic stand-by because they are also rich in other substances. At least 100 IU are required a day, but do not begin with large doses.

Vitamin E is an essential element in the prevention of premature aging, and I have also always stressed the need for older people to take good supplies of it.

A lack of vitamin E upsets the sexual life of males, and is particularly manifested in laziness, lassitude and listlessness.

Vitamin K

This vitamin is essential for the clotting of the blood. It is calcium in essence (refer to section on mineral salts). The human body can manufacture it. Milk, peanuts, soybeans and yoghurt facilitate its manufacture.

Vitamin P

This is found in lemons, particularly in the white pith and the peel. (Make sure the grower has not sprayed his crop with a deadly chemical spray, otherwise the peel may be toxic.) Vitamin P tones up the arterial and capillary system throughout the body, prevents high blood pressure; it is also found in most other citrus fruits. Sometimes this vitamin is called 'Rutin' or 'Bioflavonida'. Grapes and rose hips also contain traces of vitamin P.

Vitamin F

This is now better known as Unsaturated Fatty Acids. Generally speaking, fats are more difficult to absorb into the human digestive system than starches, but they produce twice as much heat; it is essential to reduce the consumption of fats in hot weather and hot climates. There are two kinds of fats: Unsaturated Fatty Acids (UFAs), which are safe, and the anti-vitamins known as Saturated Fatty Acids. Females need about one fifth of the UFA intake needed by males. Another factor closely interwoven with the inclusion of fats in the diet is cholesterol. Most animal oils and foods such as butter, egg yolk, lard and similar animal fats contain rich supplies of fats but lamentably rich supplies of cholesterol as well. Cholesterol can choke the arteries and damage the circulatory system which weakens not only physical performance but encourages premature aging as it becomes less efficient. Regrettably, some doctors write about the need for fats, but do not explain the difference between UFAs and SFAs. The human nervous system is rich in UFAs, and requires only UFAs. Deficiency is very prevalent in Britain and America particularly, and throughout the 'civilized' world generally.

The worst culinary habit man has is frying food, which destroys UFAs, vitamins A, E and K. There is a direct relationship between duodenal ulcers and deficiency of UFAs. Cases of psoriasis, disseminated sclerosis and ulcers have been healed by increasing UFAs in the diet.

The best sources of UFAs are wheat germ oil, corn oil,

sunflower seed oil, cotton oil, olive oil, linseed oil and halibut liver oil. It is, however, possible for a person to consume a lot of fats in the diet and still be starved of UFAs. Fat alone is not the answer; it must be the right sort of fat!

Is Your Stomach a Trash Can?

A dustbin is something into which we throw all sorts of things willy-nilly. If you throw things into your stomach in the same way you will never be healthy.

There are some foods which counteract the action of others; one example is milk. If you consume milk with biscuits, bread or cake, the calcium content of the milk forms a solid with these carbohydrate foods, from which the body cannot extract calcium.

Drinking during a meal is strongly to be advised against, for this commonly encountered habit weakens the digestive juices in the stomach, diluting them until they no longer perform their proper function adequately.

Badly combined foods can cause fermentation in the colon and the stomach; this is a form of poisoning, and produces all sorts of irritations and ulcers. Some foods produce acid in the body, and others produce alkali. The human body is well equipped to deal with both processes, but it is not very efficient at dealing with both of them at the same time. Think how often in the past you have consumed a mouthful of meat and potatoes together; a fork containing some acid-producing roast turkey and alkali-producing chestnut sauce. The combinations are endless.

Foods that produce a powerful increase of acids in the body are often most attractive for traditional reasons, but we must admit that nearly all the diseased conditions known to man thrive best in highly acid conditions in the body. To complicate matters slightly, foods which are clearly acid (such as citrus fruits) produce alkali, while those which are clearly alkali (corn, haddock, rice) produce acid! It does not follow that we should avoid all the foods which produce acid conditions, but it is unwise to consume them in conditions of weakened health.

The rule barely applies for well-built outdoor workers, who

because they are doing hard, physical work often retain more natural stomachs which can consume ostrich-like almost any combination and get away with it. However, for indoor workers, car-traveling office workers, salesmen and about 70 per cent of urban civilization, this rule is essential. For the outdoor types it need be followed exactly only if there is any sign of illness.

Here are some general instructions about the foods you can mix.

With proteins you can eat green vegetables, acid fruits and fats. There is a tendency to cook green vegetables until all nourishment in them has gone; if you must have them cooked, make sure they are only lightly steamed. Here are some dishes: fish with lemon juice; pork with apple sauce; eggs and lettuce; cheese and apples; chicken with pineapple.

With starches you may eat green vegetables, fats, sugars, dried fruits (try dried fruit sandwich). Good combinations are bread and butter; bread and honey; oats or millet with cream (in any form); salads with oil; figs, dates and bananas; mixed dried fruits in cream.

Fats combine best with sugars and acid fruits, for example: cream or butter with acid fruits; cream and Barbados sugar beaten up together; nuts and cream.

If you are in need of a wholly alkaline-producing diet, the following foods will help: almonds, apples, asparagus, bananas, beans, beets, cabbage, carrots, celery, chestnuts, kale, lemons, lettuce, limes, milk, oranges, pears, radishes.

If you need a wholly acid-producing diet for any reason, you can choose from: bread, chicken, corn, cranberries, eggs, haddock, lean meats, oatmeal, peanuts, rabbit and rice.

Eating is quite a therapy on its own. Furthermore it is one which has been comparatively neglected. It is a field in which, however, some doctors have dabbled with complete disregard for the nature of man, for example, encouraging children to drink concentrated orange juice (artificially treated) which has been shown to relate to dental decay!

18

EYE DIAGNOSIS (IRIDOLOGY)

This is fairly popular in Western Europe, but little known elsewhere. It is very effective in the hands of a trained operator, but there are many difficulties. A magnifying glass is essential.

AN ELEMENTARY CHART

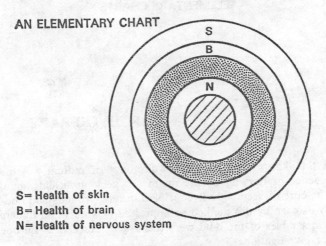

S = Health of skin
B = Health of brain
N = Health of nervous system

The attached diagrams will indicate how it works.

Any spots, cracks or marks shown against any specific area indicate that the marked area is not healthy.

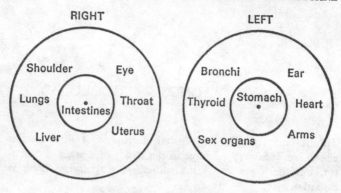

ELEMENTARY CHARTS

19.

EARTH THERAPY

A little-known fact behind the discovery of radium was the practice of burying people up to the neck in healing mud. The cure of seemingly irreducible illnesses, wounds and bodily damage by this method so impressed explorers and traders that samples of the mud were taken and returned to Europe for investigation.

There is no doubt at all that the human body can absorb mineral radiations from the earth. When we lie on the sands of the beach in the sun, silica and other radiations from the sand do us as much good as the shining rays of the Aten sun disc. Cases have been recorded of the healing of rheumatic and arthritic patients who were buried up to the neck in loose sand on a hot beach for about an hour a day for two weeks.

Apaches, Navajos and other tribes of Southwest America were well acquainted with the therapeutic properties of soil. Frank Hill, a South African farmer, discovered in 1948 a remarkable, hitherto unidentified mineral, which came to be called *Vis Vitae* because as a life force, restorative and healer it had properties of radiation that produced cures even when simply carried on the body near the troubled area. It is reddish in color, with a wavelength of 1.5 cm and a radiational figure of 75726.5 (Dr. Copen's research), which does not vary by day or night; this is very near the radiational figure for healthy human tissue. Radionic experiments indicate that it is remarkably prophylactic. Dr. N. E. Kain, writing in *Outspan*, described it as a soil that cures the sick.

There seems to be something similar in Montana called Lang's mineral powder, which I have heard of but have no further details about.

As to the credulous, see the Gospel of St. John, Chapter 9: 'And as Jesus passed by, he saw a man which was blind from his birth . . . he spat on the ground, and made clay of the spittle, and he anointed the eyes of the blind man with the clay.' The man had his sight restored.

In many forms of folk medicine clean clay (no gravel) is applied to the body (not over open wounds) for healing internal injuries, stomachaches, etc. I have no experience of this, but report it here for the record. Many have claimed cures for this treatment. The clay is usually fastened on with bandages.

20.

FASTS FOR HEALING

Various religious systems enjoin upon their believers the practice of fasting as a duty. Animals usually fast when they fall sick. Thus, fasting is a universal custom. If the drains in your house get clogged up, the first thing you do is to stop putting more materials into the pipe. Unfortunately, sick people do not always observe this logical rule. Usually a reduction of intake suffices, provided there is no serious constipation or stoppage of urine.

The initial feeling that one needs food is basically linked to habit and clock watching; it is midday, everybody else is eating; we must be hungry too. The human body often requires no food at all. Many primitive tribesmen eat only two meals a day, one in the early morning, another at night. I have read reports of tribes that ate only once a day—a large meal, of course.

Consult the section on DIETETICS before fasting. During a fast it is not necessary to refrain from simple drinks. Try honey and warm water (quite nourishing), fruit juices or China tea. One variation of fasting is consuming only fresh green vegetables, for example, watercress, mustard-and-cress, lettuce, raw chopped cabbage and grapes, with herbal or fruit drinks.

The body's inside skin needs its natural moist action to keep the functions of the body going correctly. If the tongue is coated with white or yellow 'fur,' not only is something distinctly wrong with the tongue but the whole of the inside skin. Headaches, catarrhal conditions, stomach upsets occur, and many bacteria which in normal conditions would be in a harmless balance in the body begin to multiply out of all proportion and become a nuisance. (q.v. APPLE CIDER VINEGAR; GUELPHE; SCHROTH.)

People about to fast for several days could begin with Mr. Dagnell's recommendation: one teaspoonful of slippery elm, half a cup of warm (but not boiled) milk and a teaspoonful of honey stirred vigorously into the whole. The Puritan Fathers would never have survived the first cruel winter on the continent had not American Indians showed them the nourishing properties of the slippery elm (Ulmus fulva). During fasting, avoid anything that makes you excessively tired; exhaustion is rarely therapeutic. Three days' fasting is the average period required to cleanse out the body.

21.

FINGERNAIL DIAGNOSIS

The diagnosis of health conditions from the fingernails stems from antiquity when palmists sought out the fate and future of men from their hands and the shape of their fingers. Sage observations were handed down for many generations for reliable indications of trends and the actual state of health.

In healthy people fingernails grow at a rate of about one eighth of an inch a month; less than this indicates a shortage of mineral salts and vitamins, and liability to develop conditions associated with such deficiencies (q.v. DIETETICS). The idea of cutting the fingernails is also historical.

White specks on the nails indicate a loss of calcium from the body. Whitish nails indicate a tendency to anemia (a shortage of red blood cells). If nails curve at the extremities over the fingers, respiratory diseases may be present; tubercular patients frequently show this growth. Transverse ridges running from east to west across the nails usually indicate that the person has had, or may still have, a fairly serious exhausting illness.

Few things damage a person's health as quickly as neglecting to wash the hands and fingers carefully after dirty work, or even after going to the bathroom. Strong alkali soaps should be guarded against. Women should at all times avoid using chemicals and paints on the nails which can weaken the tissue and induce toxic conditions, especially in women who are not in very good health. Brittle nails and hangnails are signs of ill health and mineral shortages. A tendency to bite the nails is a symptom of nervousness, generally a shortage of the vitamins B complex and E.

22.

FOODS THAT DECEIVE US

Bread

Bread is almost as old as civilization itself; in all civilized ruins there are traces of baking. In the British Museum I have seen bread that has survived four thousand years; mummified, dehydrated, but quite unmistakably bread. There is such bread to see at Pompeii and at other ruined cities.

Bread baking is a fundamental part of civilization. It can be stored for short periods, enabling man to use the time between preparation and consumption for civilized pursuits. The flesh and fruit eating nomad had to spend most of his life in search of food.

From Egyptian records we learn that there were over two score varieties of bread prepared and known. The Bible makes over two hundred references to bread, and nearly a score more to loaf or loaves! Archaeology shows us that the Neanderthal civilization used bread, which was probably moist, like cold porridge. The Phoenicians, Greeks and others all used bread. The Romans, it is said, needed to conquer Britain because it was the richest granary of Europe, and they needed to blend British corn with Egyptian to produce a more lasting and nutritious bread.

Bread has been made from many grains, wheat, rye, millet, etc., but one thing is fairly clear, and that is that artificial bleaching materials were never used until the early nineteenth century. However, more intelligent people began to insist upon natural, unbleached brown bread within a decade or two, and by the beginning of the twentieth century brown, natural bread was making a strong comeback and has become increasingly popular.

While it is true to say that 'Man does not live by bread alone', it is amazing really how much bread and how many different types of food made from flour products he consumes in a single week. If you begin to investigate how much bread you have eaten, how many cakes, buns, pastries, biscuits, how much macaroni, spaghetti, vermicelli and noodles you have eaten in your daily diet for the last month, you will be astounded. Not just in your own home, but in the office canteen, in restaurants, in snack bars, waiting on a railway station, each and every one of us consumes a mighty amount of flour products.

In view of the amount of the staple item of diet eaten, you will see at once how essential it is that it should be pure, wholesome and nutritious.

When I was a child first at school I had a notebook with beautiful copperplate proverbs which I was obliged to copy out in order to learn how to write; one of them was 'All that glitters is not gold,' or 'All that is colored white is not pure.'

Ivan Green, who wrote about the emotional connotations of color, pointed out that white is taken to signify purity only in some countries; in the Far East it is a color denoting mourning and death!

Bread is not normally white. Have you ever been in a country district where bread is made straight from normal, untreated whole-meal grain? It is a darkish brown in hue. This is the really nutritious bread, the stuff that kept hundreds of generations fighting fit, the stuff upon which they went out and conquered empires, on the strength of which they sailed then uncharted seas, built cities, palaces, cathedrals, the Parthenon, the Pyramids, the main source of food of the poet Homer, the Father of Medicine, Hippocrates, the source of nourishment of all the fabulous runners and athletes of old, the food of the first Olympic sportsmen!

Bakers produced a white loaf because of the emotional idea that white indicated purity. I am told that it was first invented at the French Court, where what was pleasing to the eye was frequently chosen instead of the solid, healthy and sensible.

For many years bread was bleached with agene, chemically known as nitrogen trichloride (NCl_3), a substance used in poison gases, a well-known nerve poison. It was many decades before the outcry raised by dietitians and natural food exponents was heeded, but by then several generations had been literally poisoned by the bad but 'pretty' bread.

Experiments in which animals were fed on an agene-bread diet led to rapid deterioration of health, fits and death. One would think that the commercial baking houses would have learned from these experiments, and from the popular outcry against agene as a bleaching agent in bread, but no!

Currently, white bread is unnaturally bleached with yet another chemical, chlorine dioxide ($Cl\ O_2$). I should mention that in the First World War chlorine was another poison gas which produced blindness and death, although I am not suggesting that the quantities of this derivative of chlorine will have the same effects. The question is whether we need go on with this ridiculous eye appeal instead of taste appeal in order to sell bread.

The adulteration of bread and flour is by no means new. It is a despicable idea to do this to some universally needed household items of diet which millions of people must have to eat, and pocket the difference. Many substances are removed from the flour before it is made into white bread. Sometimes these are replaced with cheaper chemical substitutes and the original, natural nutrients are sold back to the public at high prices.

Roman history contains some references to bakers who adulterated bread and were severely (and lethally) punished for their crime. In a historical paper for a learned society some years ago on the subject of the 'Nika Riot' in Constantinople (A.D. 532), I noted that one of the significant contributory factors was the literally poisonous bread being sold by the bakeries owned by that wily politician and unscrupulous scoundrel, John of Cappadocia.

You must seek out stone-ground whole-meal bread, and get cakes and biscuits made with stone-ground whole-meal flour. Stone-ground flour contains flakes of the real wheat germ, which look like tiny pieces of straw but are full of essential vitamins and nutrients.

Here are some statistics for the reader who likes to see things in black and white.

	White flour	Whole-meal flour
Vitamin B1	0.27 mg / 100 g	0.37 mg / 100 g
Vitamin B2	1.9	5.0
Iron	1.9	3.6
Protein %	12	13.5

Note: 28.35 g equals 1 ounce.

But as the white flour is only 70 per cent extraction, and the brown whole-meal flour is 100 per cent extraction, the figures on the left-hand side are in fact less than they look.

Bread is one of the main suppliers of carbohydrates, the substances that provide our bodies with energy. Brown flour contains about twenty grams of carbohydrate per ounce. This is a high proportion, so to cut down bread intake may rob you of energy. You must only alter the quality of the bread you eat, not omit it. White bread contains only fifteen grams of carbohydrate per ounce!

There are four types of flour commonly milled: wheat germ is rich in essential fatty acids, which means that the mineral, vitamin and protein content of this bread is the highest; whole-meal flour contains the whole grain, endosperm, husk and wheat germ in natural proportions; brown flour contains some endosperm, some husk and some of the wheat germ; white flour contains the endosperm only, is bleached, and usually has some chemical additives to preserve the flour longer, prevent damage to the product if kept under refrigeration, etc.

If you cannot obtain naturally stone-ground, homemade bread, you could eat Hovis bread which contains a high protein percentage, a high wheat-germ rate and usually more vitamin B than other factory-made bread.

Natural bread is often more expensive than white bread. The reason is that it has not been treated to keep for long periods, so consequently the baker of natural bread stands to lose money if his stock is not used up. (A standing order may be necessary at such bakers because not many shops can afford to order many more loaves than regular customers ask for.) If you look askance at spending a few more pennies a day, ask yourself how much you value your health.

The following chemicals are used by various bakeries

selling white bread: ammonium persulphate, chlorine, chlorine dioxide, potassium bromate. Do not be misled when you
learn that these are added only in 'minute' quantities. A minute quantity of cyanide can kill you; as much anthrax to go
on a pinhead will kill off a whole family! The substances
named are relatively 'harmless' only if you are prepared to
drag through life at the end of the line, last in the race, listless, lacking in vital energy.

Here is a recipe for home-baked bread. This is the bread I
bake myself. I like it, and I am sure you will.

Ingredients: 1¾ pounds stone-ground whole-meal flour; a
generous pinch of biochemically balanced salt; up to one pint
of lukewarm water; a teaspoonful of dark brown sugar; a
generous half ounce of yeast.

Use a clean bowl (not plastic); mix your flour with the
salt. Put the yeast into a glass, add the sugar, half fill the glass
with lukewarm water. Within a short time the yeast will froth
up and be ready to use. Make a space in the middle of the
bowl of flour. Pour into this space the yeast mixture and all
the water, slowly stirring while you do it.

You certainly do not have to knead the mixture. I gave up
kneading for such small amounts, and I have never failed to
get excellent bread. I simply whip briskly with a fork or a
spoon.

When the mixture has a creamy texture, cover the bowl
with a layer of wax paper, and over that place a clean towel
or cloth, keeping the bowl in a warm place for about two
hours. You will see the dough rise dramatically. When it is
nearly twice the size of the original amount, prepare one large
or two small baking tins by greasing the inside of the tins
(do not use too much grease). Then transfer the whole of
the dough into the tin or tins, allow it to rise again, using the
same paper or cloth to cover it.

When the dough has risen again for the second time, place
the tins immediately into a hot oven, and leave them there for
about three-quarters of an hour, but during the last fifteen
minutes turn the gas down slowly to prevent the sides and
crust from burning.

If your loaf is thoroughly baked you will be able to get a
distinct hollow sound from it when you tap it lightly all over

with a knife or a fork. Test the bottom of the loaf first. If you do not get a hollow sound, there is nothing for it but to put the loaf back in its tin and bake for a few minutes more.

Sugar

Nobody can be well unless he has access to plenty of oxygen. Any foodstuff that consumes oxygen and gives a poor output of energy in return is one we should avoid. White sugar, commonly eaten all over the civilized world, is a positive menace. It consumes oxygen at a most alarming rate. Avoid it!

The sugar cane grows somewhat like a familiar bamboo; it may grow as high as sixteen feet. The extracted sugar is less than 20 per cent of the weight of the cane, which is smashed and sprayed with water. Allowing for impurities the amount of sugar remaining for use is about one eighth of this total. The mixture is placed in spinners, so arranged that the chief essence, known as black molasses, is drained off. This is a highly beneficial substance, and it is pure, wholesome, very rich in mineral salts, specifically calcium, copper, manganese, potassium. Molasses contains phosphoric acid, an irreplaceable basic requirement for the health of the nervous system, and all the vitamin B group except B^1.

The trouble is that the product which is most commonly known is not the raw, powerful, healthy molasses, but the weakened sugar, which becomes paler and paler as it gets weaker.

What do you, the consumer, get for all the expensive processes of refining, other than a 'pretty' product? Is there any vitamin B left in it? Is there any vitamin left in it at all? Is there any calcium, copper, manganese or potassium left in it? The answer to each and every one of these questions is in the negative. You are paying more for a product containing less! From sugar you can get calories, a sweet-tasting carbohydrate. If 100 grams of molasses and sugar are compared, sugar contains double the amount of calories contained in black molasses. There is one mg of calcium in sugar as compared with 260 mg in black molasses; and there is less than half a milligram of potassium in sugar, whereas black molasses contains three thousand times that amount!

Sugar resembles a drug and modern civilization tends to get only one taste in all foods—'sweet.' Marco Polo refers to the Chinese using a crude natural sugar, and it is said that the ancient Egyptians, shortly before their decline, took to using sugar instead of honey.

The process of 'refining' sugar from sugar beets is, in essence, the same, so that most goodness is usually removed with the 'tops' of the plant which are turned into cattle food. This is done frequently in the field before the plants reach the factory; thus the plant's natural defenses against bacteria are destroyed even before it gets to the 'refinery'. A very learned friend of mine maintains that one of the surest signs of decline in civilization is when people cease to use words correctly, when they use words with double meanings or a falsely transposed meaning, as is the word 'refined' in the food industry.

Now let us look at the ways in which sugar is consumed: in drinks such as tea, coffee, cocoa, chocolate, soft drinks, ice creams, biscuits, cakes, sweets and much else. You would be really shocked if you could take off time to add up how much sugar you are consuming every day! Ask yourself how your tongue can perform its natural function of distinguishing by taste whether food is good or bad when you flavor everything with the same sweet taste?

White sugar penetrates through the wall of the stomach without being digested, and can create a state of imbalance in calcium-phosphorus ratio in the body. White sugar actually damages the natural blood sugar content of the body and thus can facilitate the development of disorders of the pancreas gland and the nervous system. Everybody needs a nervous system in good condition in order to attain peak performance.

Try using honey instead of sugar. I have spoken to beekeepers in high Aragon, in the wilds of the Crna Gora, and in pleasant wooded dales of Sjaelland; they have, I find, all of them, a wisdom, an air of peace, and above all a tremendous understanding of the ways of the bees.

I am told that honey, four thousand years old and more, was found in the tombs of the ancient Egyptian Pharaohs, completely free from bacteria of any sort, still edible! In botanic medicine, it is commonly known as a powerful antiseptic. I have myself, when faced with a cut or wound, often placed 100 per cent pure untreated honey (straight from the hive) onto the wound, placed a light dressing over it, and seen it heal up clean without any scar or secondary infection! The secret is that honey absorbs moisture, and secondary infections need moisture to develop. Indeed many doctors from the time of Hippocrates have recommended honey. In addition to mineral salts it also contains the essential vitamins for sportsmen: vitamins C, E and A.

Because of the habit of spraying crops and flowers with DDT and similar dangerous sprays (as listed in Rachel Carson's *Silent Spring*), it is advisable to avoid honey from the civilized countries, and take by preference honey imported from the falsely named more 'primitive' areas, where the pollen collected by the bees is uncontaminated by man-made insecticides, which are already showing such disastrous, and in some cases lethal, results for man himself.

There are many other sources of sweetness: dried bananas, dried figs, dates, raisins, fresh fruits, sultanas, etc. But when buying fruit, take care to wash it before eating, just in case somebody has sprayed it. Best of all, try to buy only from sources where no sprays or man-made chemicals are in use, then you are safe.

I remember the dark green honey I used to buy from the wonderful old beekeeper I knew as a boy; how rich and healthy it tasted. I can promise any sportsman who takes honey a really noticeable improvement in performance after only a week. I still do a little weightlifting (among other pursuits) and always take a spoonful of honey first.

Honey contains the following mineral salts: calcium, chlorine, copper, iron, magnesium, manganese, phosphorus, potassium, silicon and sodium.

23.

FOOT ZONE THERAPY
(REFLEXOLOGY)

This is an ancient Chinese form of therapy that has recently been rediscovered. The ends of the limbs are significantly sensitive parts of the human organism. For thousands of years men have known that the hands are maps of the individual's character and of his potential. Likewise it is ancient knowledge that the feet are a map of the individual's state of physical balance.

Everyone knows that the soles of the feet are very sensitive. Through them he is connected with the earth, and one possibility why walking barefoot on grass is so soothing is that the earth's energy may be able to balance the body's energies which are manifested on the soles of the feet. Another idea is that the earth can drain one's negativity through the feet is perhaps less convincing. Although the practice of wearing shoes insulates us from the therapeutic value of being "earthed" to earth energy, the fact that we do wear shoes makes our feet more sensitive, and amenable to foot, or zone, therapy!

There is a correspondence in this sense between the principle of acupuncture and the principle of zone therapy. For, as the illustration shows, specific areas of the soles of the feet seem to relate to individual organic functions. If an organ loses its state of balance with the whole organism, a sensitive nodule can form in its specific area. Practiced manipulation or massage of this spot will lead to quick relief of the imbalance, just as a needle inserted or manipulated in the specific acupuncture point corresponding to the organ will bring the organ into balance.

The attraction of foot therapy is that you can experiment with it on yourself. Also, it is not a difficult technique to learn

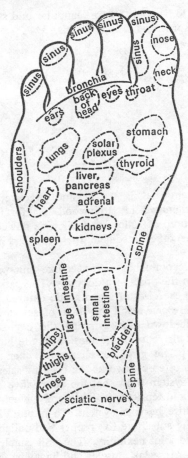

to apply to others, and a beginner can do no harm. It has recently become quite popular in the United States, where many doctors, both allopathic and non-allopathic, practice it. It is very useful for diagnosis, for if any point when pressed down firmly with the thumb is unduly sensitive, this indicates the need for treatment to help that part of the body. As a therapy it is also effective in alleviating many conditions: sinusitis, indigestion, sciatica and muscular tensions. Specialists claim also to be able to cure glandular and stomach troubles, sexual disorders and appendicitis.

24.

GRAVITONICS

This is a system that is taught and practiced mainly in America. It originated in Hollywood, California. It is for those who are tired of following a doctor's advice to take an aspirin or some other medicine for their bad back, spinal pains, etc.

The system recommends a trapeze-like unit which can be fixed in between the posts of a doorway. The patient is taught how to perform exercises of a gymnastic nature on this, nothing strenuous. He can reach the stage of suspending himself (herself) upside-down, and gripping the bar and supports with the legs. This reduces the tension in the lumbar region and gives the pelvic girdle a chance to change the body weight which so often overworks the back muscles. The practitioners of the system show that the cumulative effect of everyday weights and tensions do not merely affect the muscles but also the entire nervous system. To quote Victor Steele, 'There is no drug substitute for proper body alignment, good muscle tone, and joint flexibility.' The unit enables the pelvis to rotate backwards, relax muscles and ligaments, and encourages elasticity in bodily movements.

Lack of exercise weakens muscles. Increased emotional stresses makes muscles tense up unnaturally; emotions are so often expressed by muscular responses.

The system seems to be gaining in popularity.

25.

GUELPHE FAST

This is fundamentally the opposite of SCHROTH THERAPY or cure (*q.v.*). It is an easier fast in many ways, but each of them has its own benefits.

The Guelphe fast allows you to drink nutrient substances of a pure and natural kind but it does not permit you to touch any solid or semisolid foods at all. Fruit juices, vegetable juices and broths are allowed, but no pieces of vegetable in the broth.

One variation of the cure is to drink pure white wine, and I tried this once (with guilty feelings of pleasure) and found it very effective indeed. St. Paul recommended wine even if Mahomet didn't!

The advantage of the Guelphe fast is that it lends itself to a large number of variations suggested by dietetics: for example, a predominance of lettuce juice, carrot juice, herbal teas, etc. (See DIETETICS and HERBALISM, etc.)

The cure can certainly be used for two days without interruption, but twenty-four hours is generally long enough to be effective. Often alternate Schroth and Guelphe fasts are recommended by nature cure consultants.

26

HAPPINESS CURE

The ancient Chinese sometimes applied a method of therapy which approaches the psychosomatic ideas popular since the researches of Dr. Flanders Dunbar and others. The Orientals thought that the basis of all disease was unhappiness. Thus to make the patient happy again was to restore him to health. This has limitations, of course, for what would satisfy the dearest wish of a sick patient might make everybody else within range most unhappy. It is not just a simple matter of hedonistic satisfaction, but rather a need for the patient to come to terms with life. None of us can have everything he or she wants, and the more negative the personality the more it wishes to be made happy, rather than to act positively to create happiness. In John Masefield's words: 'Happiness is not what you find, it's what you make. The days that make us happy make us wise.'

An untutored child wants parents to amuse it, to make it laugh, to find it games to play: a happy child makes its own games, its own fun, its own world. Regrettably some adults never grow up in the true meaning of the words; they remain children at heart, unable to cope with problems of life.

When I was a boy men roamed the wintry streets with bells in their hands, trays of muffins on their heads; some men spent their days lighting the gas lamps. He who owned a bicycle was king indeed. Of course I do not mean that what were relatively poor times were good, but I emphasize that it is easier to be happy when wants are few and easily satisfied. It is when one has enough money to buy a fifteen-foot yacht, and feels one cannot live without a forty-five-foot one, that life opens up new complications.

There is nothing wrong in ambition, only wrong in the way we react to it. A great deal of disease may be born in the frustration of ambitions. How many people do I know who are sick solely because they feel that their life has become purposeless, that nothing has succeeded! The psychologist Harold I. Smith wrote:

Most people today are so busy running away from themselves that they have not a clue what self-awareness is. The fact that so many people today pass their lives away without ever getting to know themselves is not surprising. Many people are literally scared to be alone and quiet, when they might have to face up to themselves. What they see is too devastating for their morale. During their waking hours what time is left over after they have obtained enough money to exist upon is spent either going to the races, sports, parties, dancing, playing cards, watching TV, and so on. What hope for people who waste their lives of ever getting to know themselves, of attaining self-awareness, or of building a truly successful life!

Is it possible, we may ask, for a person to be truly happy who does not know himself or herself, who does not really understand what is required to make the personality radiate with happiness, because there is no true awareness of what the real personality constitutes?

I remember how Madame Marie Rambert once told me, many years ago, that Nijinsky, one of the greatest dancers of living memory, was a very inarticulate person, that nearly all his expressions of self were transmitted through dancing rather than through speech. Marie was, in those days, very much in love with the fabulous dancer; perhaps if this kindly, cultured, Warsaw-born genius had married him, his fate would have been less sad.

Some people can find happiness expressing themselves through sewing, painting, playing the piano, dancing, a thousand and one different ways. The secret of the cure is to help the patient discover what his or her true personality is, and to teach him how to express that personality in a way that satisfies, ennobles and increases his standing, worth and value in the community in which he lives. In this sense that a person who knows himself is free of frustrations and aware of how he may contribute to the society in which he lives finds a new happiness, the old Chinese treatment is quite true. What may be misleading is the too facile translation of the Chinese word for happiness. The pictographic script of the old Celestial Kingdom (as it liked to call itself) contained several ways of expressing happiness. One was composed of a man, a bowl of rice and a field from which ever more food could come.

This reminds me of the lady visiting China some decades ago. She became very popular with the local people, although she never succeeded in learning to read the language. When she left they presented her with a handbag and told her that it was inscribed with the message: 'May you always be happy.'

The lady was very proud of this, and carried it on many social events. On one occasion a missionary who had lived many years in China saw the bag, asked her if she knew what the writing said. She explained that it signified a wish that she should always be happy. In a way it does, replied the cleric, although word for word it says: 'May you become the mother of countless children!'

R. L. Stevenson said: 'There is an idea abroad among moral people that they should make their neighbours good. One person that I have to make good and that is myself. My duty to my neighbour is much more clearly expressed by the saying that I have made him happy—if I may.'

27

HERBALISM

This is the oldest known method of healing the sick. It outdates practically every other known form of therapy.

History

The oldest record hitherto revealed is Chinese; it is the *Pen Tsao*, dating about 3000 B.C., in which about a thousand remedies are listed. It owes its origin to the Emperor Sheng Noong who seems to have been one of the great culture-founding figures which legends describe. He is credited with the invention of the plow, the establishment of agriculture and teaching people to cultivate rice. He is said to be the man who discovered the medicinal value of cinnamon. The bark of the mulberry tree and the roots of rhubarb and many other plants figured on the list of the herbalist Emperor.

Medicine without morals has many drawbacks, one of which emerging from the Chinese pharmacopoeia was the use of opium. Modern herbalists have a very strict approach to healing, and employ no herb that could possibly have any ill or side effect.

Thousands of miles distant, human experience had also discovered, independently, the value of herbs for therapy. The ancient Egyptians set up their House of Life to which sick people were taken for restoration to health. If their condition was judged to be beyond repair, they were removed to the House of Death and trained how to meet the end of their bodies, how to behave when entering the spirit world, what etiquette to follow when meeting spirits, etc.

Olive oil, cloves, myrrh, castor oil and many other herbs in common use today were first used in the Egyptian civilization and in the Babylonian-Assyrian cultures. The knowledge of herbal healing grew together in the two cultures because commercial bonds linked them and we know that herbs formed part of their trade.

As far as we are able to judge, essential oils were first used in ancient Egypt. I am told that when the tombs were opened some of the pottery still bore traces of perfumed herbal oils.

Among the achievements of the Greeks was a unique codification of knowledge which forms the basis of the science of medicine. The principal figure in this work was Hippocrates of Cos. His father may have been a priest of Aesculapius, whose holy snakes are frequently used as a symbol of medicine even today.

Hippocrates is said to have spent his youth reading the case histories inscribed on tablets in the temple, and his knowledge was sufficient to save the city of Athens from a disastrous plague. He was a most careful physician who used herbs, dietetics and exercise to restore the body to health. He is the first man to have explored psychosomatic medicine. Hippocrates was most guarded in his use of surgery; he taught that a cancer which is cut by a surgeon is less likely to be wholly healed than one which is dissolved away by herbs, change of diet, psychosomatic treatment, etc.

Until the turn of the twentieth century the majority of healing throughout the world had a herbal basis. During earlier centuries the people who used toad's skin, chemicals from metals and the like in healing were regarded as magicians, alchemists or quacks. The reasons for turning away from herbs were religious and political. The earliest herbal writings were of pagan origin; there were references to Apollo, Aesculapius, and so on, which the politicians who needed a common religion to bring together people who had no racial unity within the Roman Empire, found embarrassing. The Christians found references to the older Aryan religion intolerable, and so encouragement was given to those who were prepared to look for new types of healing. (In the same way two centuries later Stalin gave preferment to Lysenko's biologically impossible conception of botany because it seemed to support Communist party dogma.) The suffering that this imposed on humanity would have been all the greater except that herbalists seem throughout history to have been genuine healers, filled with compassion for their patients. Unlike the medical school of allopathy, as practiced in universities and hospitals today, they published in simple language their knowledge of herbs and healing so that all who could read might seek, find, apply and heal. If a few errors in judgment seem to have accumulated here and there, this is often because nowadays we know too little of the conditions and semantics of their times. Nicholas Culpeper (1616–54), for example, advocated astrological indications. However, his *Complete Herbal* (still available in a facsimile edition) was a significant figure contribution to the development of herbalism because he published for all the world to see the entire pharmacopoeia of the medical profession of his day. This greatly enraged his colleagues although it provided health for the poor who could go out and search out their herbs freely.

Herbalism is one form of healing that it is virtually impossible to control because anybody with a book can go out and collect the plants for himself, make the medicines and take them, with the secure knowledge that he is experimenting but following upon the lines that kept man alive and well for thousands of years.

In the nineteenth century, especially in America, herbalism became a powerful alternative to the healing based upon inorganic metals, and much else which passed as allopathy. Samuel Thomson (1769–1843) so upset New Hampshire doctors that they persuaded the state legislature to pass a law specifically naming him, not for practicing medicine 'illegally' (the usual term with which to charge non-allopathic practitioners), but to prevent him healing people without charging them. It did them no good. Thomson's school, and men such as Samuel Tilke (1794–?), produced astoundingly safe, efficient cures from herbal medicines.

Now on both sides of the Atlantic Ocean, millions of people have turned to herbal medicine, or as it is frequently called now, botanic medicine, in preference to all other forms of healing. Attempts have been made to hustle herbalists into unions and associations to avoid state displeasure and persecution. Many governments are persuaded that allopathy is the only form of healing and that all other healers should be committed to an *auto-da-fé*. Thousands of herbalists, however, remain independent. By refusing to name the condition they treat to the patient and by insisting that they are providing restorative teas, they cannot be attacked. Many excellent books for the identification of symptoms are available nowadays, and courses in herbal healing are available even by correspondence. Of course this does not exclude the need to learn anatomy, physiology, dietetics and some psychology, all of which go hand in hand with any form of healing.

It is a criticism of the twentieth century that good therapists must claim they are merely giving friends and relatives a nice cup of tea like Grandmother used to make to avoid being hauled through the courts by an established clique whose theories pass as facts because nobody bothers to investigate them.

Modern Herbalism

Herbal medicine works upon the natural theory of correcting what is wrong with the body so that it may heal itself. It seeks to strengthen the natural functions of the body. Most herbs are classified into groups that singly or jointly bring about these results.

A list is appended here. Clearly, nobody should pick out a herb and use it without reading up on its functions, how it was used by herbalists historically, how much and how often, etc.

Alteratives. These may be classed as unidentified vitamins, hormones and mineral salts. In a manner largely unknown to us they can alter serious illnesses to produce cures. Examples: blue flag (*Iris versicolor*); burdock root (*Arctium lappa*); red clover flowers (*Trifolium pratense*); yellow dock (*Rumex crispus*).

Anthelmintics. These expel worms and parasites inhabiting the intestines, for example: balmony (*Chelone glabra*); male fern (*Aspidium felix mas*); wormwood (*Artemisia absinthium*).

Astringents. These increase the firmness of the mucous membranes and skin, and check excessive secretions. They are valuable also as gargles, lotions, mouthwashes and external

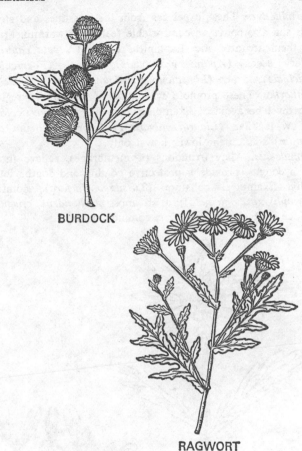

BURDOCK

RAGWORT

washes. Examples: agrimony (*Agrimonia eupatoria*); black alder bark (*Alnus glutinosa*); goldenrod (*Solidago virgaurea*); hawthorn berries (*Crataegus oxyacantha*); sage (*Salvia officinalis*).

Calmatives. Excellent to take as a warm tea before retiring, for example: catnip (*Nepeta cataria*); camomile flowers (*Anthemis nobilis*); fennelseed (*Foeniculum officinale*); linden flowers (*Tilia europaea*).

Carminatives. These expel gas from the intestines and stomach and also convey a comfortable feeling of warmth. Many of them are aromatic. Examples: catnip (*Nepeta cataria*); celery seeds (*Apium graveolans*); fennel (*Foeniculum officinale*); lovage (*Ligusticum livisticum*).

Cathartics. These promote evacuation of the bowels; regular use must be avoided. Examples: blue flag (*Iris versicolor*); yellow toadflax (*Linaria vulgaris*). Rhubarb (*Rheum palmatum*) acts on the lower bowel only.

Demulcents. Allay irritations of membranes, relieve throat from coughs, provide a protective coating and soothe internally. Examples: coltsfoot (*Tussilago farfara*); comfrey (*Symphytum officinale*); Irish moss (*Chondrus crispus*); quince seed (*Pyrus cydonia*); common oatmeal.

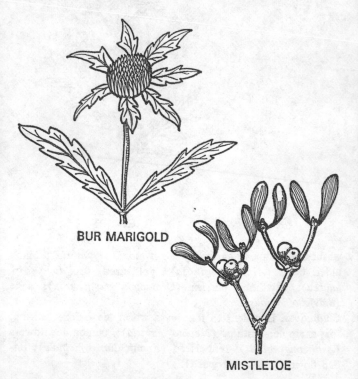

BUR MARIGOLD

MISTLETOE

Diaphoretics. Encourage the expulsion of toxins by sweating. It is best to take them either before going to bed or when not needing to go out into cold air. Examples: blessed thistle (*Carduus benedictus*); catnip; camomile; elder flowers; pennyroyal (*Mentha pulegium*); ragwort (*Senecio aureus*); yarrow (*Achillea millefolium*).

Diuretics. Increase the expulsion of urine together with toxins. If effect is required urgently take the diuretic on rising (when the stomach is empty). Examples: bilberry leaves (*Vaccinium myrtillus*); broom tops (*Cytisus scoparius*), also useful against dropsy and gallstones; horsetail grass (*Equisetum hiemale*); parsley (*Petroselinum sativum*).

Expectorants. Loosen phlegm and coatings of the mucous membranes. Examples: coltsfoot (*Tussilago farfara*); elecampane (*Inula helenium*); maidenhair fern (*Adiantum capillus-veneris*).

Nervines. Relax from strain, excitement and tension, for example, camomile; catnip; yarrow.

Stimulants. Quicken the functions of the body. The effect of any stimulant on an excitable person is never as beneficial as upon calmer people; also their effect upon people who habitually drink alcohol is less beneficial than upon sober people. Examples: goldenrod; pennyroyal; yarrow.

Vulneraries. To be applied to cuts, minor wounds, etc. As most plants contain rich deposits of chlorophyll, almost any green leaves can be applied to an open wound. The following have been recommended by herbalists through the ages; mistletoe (*Viscum album*); marigold (*Calendula officinalis*); self-heal (*Prunella vulgaris*).

There are, of course, thousands of other herbs and very many other functional classifications.

One of the fallacies advanced by allopaths is that herbs are too primitive, raw, impure and weak to be effective, and that they are only usable when they have been concentrated, refined, turned into quintessential extracts and so on. This is nonsense. The human body when unwell is far better able to make use of weaker doses than stronger doses, because the herbalist is not seeking to kill germs but to nourish the body. It is ridiculous to claim that he must do this the same way as the soi-disant orthodox physicians do. If a man has exhaustion and thirst after crossing the Gobi Desert you do not let him gulp down copious draughts of water; far from it, he is made to take frequent small sips, since if he drank deeply he would die. If you take a man with frostbite into a room and put him right up against a powerful stove he too would die; he must be warmed gently and massaged slowly. So much for ill-informed criticism of herbal methods.

There is a difference between primitive herbalism and modern herbalism. Originally, healing was effected by the use, in one form or another, of one herb. The tendency over the last couple of centuries has been to mix herbs. I do mix some myself, but I prefer to use most herbs as simples. I strongly recommend to the beginner and the layman in general that he or she use only one herb unless a book gives specific directions to mix them. Never mix herbs at random! A sick animal always selects one herb to chew for its cure, not half a dozen.

Old Herbal Recipes

Herbal teas are generally made as follows. For a pleasant, refreshing tea, use one or two teaspoonfuls to an ordinary teapot filled afterward with boiling water. For therapeutical purposes use one ounce to one pint of boiling water. In each case the herb is used *dried*, not fresh. Fresh herbs are much stronger, and should always be washed in slightly salted water before use (to clear off any insects). No beginner should use fresh herbs. Some traditional recipes are given below, but if the reader collects herbs, every care should be taken to carry a flower identification book, and use it most assiduously. Never take a chance; if you cannot identify a plant precisely and exactly, leave it. Leaves are used unless otherwise specified.

Acidity: Peppermint tea with lemon juice; mellitot tea.

Anemia: Stinging nettle tea.

Antiseptics: Witch hazel, garlic, onion.

Appetite, Loss of: Caraway, celery, horseradish, rhubarb, watercress, all eaten rather than made up as teas.

Asthma: Coltsfoot, honeysuckle, agrimony and mullein.

Bladder Troubles: Asparagus (eaten), betony, goldenrod, horsetail grass.

Bleeding, to Stop: Apply nettle juice externally.

Blood Cleansers: Burdock (seeds or roots), clover, dandelions, horsetail grass, watercress.

Bruises: Apply comfrey or crushed sage leaves, and bandage on lightly.

Catarrh: Equal parts of elderflower, peppermint and yarrow: a cupful every hour when the symptoms are first suspected. If possible chew one small clove of garlic every two hours.

Colic: Half-strength thyme or caraway seed tea.

Constipation: Slippery elm and honey: one teaspoonful of each in a cup of hot water before breakfast every morning.

Coughs: Coltsfoot and mullein tea (equal parts).

Diarrhea: Blackberry or silverweed tea.

Eyebath: One teaspoonful of witch hazel to three teaspoonfuls of water (use a clean eyebath before applying to the eyes every morning).

Female Troubles: Camomile tea, hollyhock or motherwort tea, mugwort.

Flu: Yarrow tea with lemon juice and honey. Chew garlic.

Gums, to Strengthen: Chew lemon skin (do not swallow it).

Hair Conditioners: Use same strength as for teas: camomile, nettles, quince (juice), rosemary, thyme.

High Blood Pressure: Take celery, hawthorn leaf or rosemary tea in preference to tea or coffee.

Insomnia: Take a teaspoonful of honey, a cupful of hot fresh milk and a pinch of cinnamon before retiring for the night.

Jaundice: Take agrimony, fennel or tansy tea in preference to ordinary tea and coffee.

Kidney Complaints: Eat plenty of asparagus and celery, drink elderflower or tansy teas. Follow dietetic advice.

Laxatives: Honey and hot water upon rising; fennel, licorice, rhubarb (boiled stalks, eaten); rose jam.

Liver Complaints: Dandelion, rosemary, soapwort, St. John's wort, tansy, wood betony.

Menstruation Difficulties: Camomile tea (one of the oldest remedies), lady's mantle, mint, wood sorrel, yarrow.

Nausea: Equal parts of tansy and peppermint, as a tea.

Nervous Complaints: Sage tea with a half-teaspoonful of basil added; balm melissa tea; peppermint and rosemary tea.

Pharyngitis: Cherry juice and honey in warm water, some drunk and some gargled.

Pregnancy: Raspberry leaf tea (half ounce to one pint of boiling water) drunk daily for three months before labor, is said to ease parturition.

Rheumatic Complaints: There are very many types of rheumatism, but most of them are eased if wood betony tea with honey, or nettle tea with a few birch leaves and honey, is drunk instead of ordinary tea or coffee.

Scalp Troubles: Massage in a 'tea' of rosemary with lemon juice added.

Shock: Sage tea with a pinch of basil.

Tonics: Caraway seed, celery, centaury, ground ivy, peppermint, tansy and yarrow.

28.

HOMEOPATHY

This is one branch of healing that has made its peace with the orthodox medical school, and has found itself almost buried because of it. All the early homeopaths were allopaths, and the emotional need for union with the parental medical world was too strong for them.

In recent years there have appeared a number of well-trained and efficient homeopaths who have nothing to do with the established allopaths. It seems that only through these loners will homeopathy survive. One of the conditions of 'recognition' has been that all homeopaths should first be trained as allopaths before they begin to study homeopathy. Few men can afford to begin studying again after the six-year allopathic course.

The unwieldy word homeopathy is the anglicization of the original German *ö* as *oe;* originally it was called *Hom-*

öopathie. The Germans have contributed much to the healing arts, for instance, Schüssler, Semelweiss, Virchow, Liebig, Kneipp and Samuel Hahnemann.

In 1796, C. F. Samuel Hahnemann published in the *Journal der praktischen Arzneikunst* an essay upon the principle of discovering new therapeutics. The results of his research appeared further in more complete form in 1810 with the publishing of his *Organon der Heilkunst.* This so incensed the established medical profession that he was dismissed from his post as lecturer of the University of Leipzig. Fortunately Ferdinand, the Duke of Anhalt Köthen, invited Hahnemann to be court physician. Hahnemann died in Paris after his retirement from the court in 1843. Over the years he had published still further works, and gathered an enthusiastic number of students around him who proclaimed his gospel of homeopathy. Among his most famous books were *Die reine Arzneimittellehre,* 1822 (six volumes), and *Die chronischen Krankheiten,* 1828 (four volumes).

What was so revolutionary about Hahnemann's work? Firstly, his principle that like cures like. The fundamental idea of the treatment is to find a substance that produces almost exactly the same symptoms as the patient displays; this is then administered. The growth of homeopathy has stemmed from the speed and effectiveness with which cures take place. Here is a simple example. I was knocked off a bicycle by a car that was cutting a corner carelessly. My left knee, though fortunately not broken, was badly injured and swelled up very badly. I was taken by ambulance immediately after the accident to the London Homoeopathic Hospital, and one of the specifics which they gave me was made from a bee sting. Now this normally causes a swelling, and yet it is capable of reducing one! How does it work?

Homeopathic medicine is not given to cure the disease or condition, but to stimulate the vital force to function efficiently. What we call disease is a decline of the vital force caused by anxiety, cold, eating too much, drinking too much, exhaustion, shock, absorbing polluted air, drink, food, liquids, fumes, etc. When the tone of the vital force has been lowered, many things come out of balance, bacterial growth may find conditions favorable to increase, glands may produce too little or too much of their secretions; a thousand things may go awry. In view of the unique methods involved, the homeopathic pharmacopoeia is one of the largest in the world.

The second difference in approach to healing is the law of direction of healing: curing the internal condition first, the outward last; from above downwards, from the most vital organs affected to the lesser ones.

The third difference is one which in the light of modern experience is far more understandable than it was at the time Hahnemann first taught it. He taught that the smaller the potency of the drug administered, the more easily it was absorbed by the sick body, which rejected strong doses. The system is to place one drop of the actual substance used for healing the patient's condition in ninety-nine drops of spirit. This is mechanically shaken to produce a distribution of the properties. From this concoction is taken one drop, which is placed with a further ninety-nine parts, shaken. The process is repeated, usually six times, and sometimes twelve times. One part of a mineral substance is pounded with nine parts of milk sugar; one part is taken and pounded with nine parts of milk sugar, and so on. The number of extractions is marked by the figures 6X or 12X on the label. The more diluted the material becomes in the ultimate dose the higher, it is claimed, is the effect upon the vital force.

One may conclude that such a skilled and complicated method of healing requires specialization, and has little to learn from established medical practice.

Remarkable cures have been recorded with this treatment since it was first instituted. Many medicines in several branches of healing are administered too strongly. A sick body can make better use of small doses administered more frequently than it can of giant, powerful doses shoved down the gullet like a knockout blow to a boxer. In my works on herbal medicine I frequently advise, and do myself administer, doses about half the strength that many other practitioners of botanic medicine recommend. I have found this a safer and more efficient method of healing.

One of the interesting facts of homeopathic research was the willingness of Hahnemann and his associates to experiment upon themselves. Behind their research was the theory that whatever made sick could heal.

Thomas Sydenham, the 'English Hippocrates' (1624–89), had been one of the first writers to maintain that a disease was not attacking the body but the body's method of curing itself of something that was going wrong.

Hahnemann proposed that an illness had to be studied and understood, not just destroyed. His enlightened attitude was not shared by medical colleagues whose income depended rather upon mystification. They ridiculed him, but their cousins the chemists, seeing in the cheap, homeopathic remedies financial collapse, banded together in righteous wrath—to little avail, for nothing succeeds like success.

In France and Germany it took root. In England it became popular to some extent, especially among the wealthy aristocrats who were weary of the failure of allopathy to cure.

One aspect of Hahnemann's teaching was that each patient is a different case, and that the physician must treat the patient and not the disease. The application of this idea to herbal medicine has helped me considerably in my own work, and it is a logical application for any healing art. We all owe much to Hahnemann.

29.

HYPNOSIS FOR HEALING
AND DIAGNOSIS

An old tomb at Thebes shows on a bas-relief carving an Egyptian priest hypnotizing a patient. The traditions of the ancient Greeks and Romans, as well of those of China, all refer to the use of hypnotism to relieve pain.

The Moorish physician Avicenna taught that the mind of man could not only act upon his own body, but upon other bodies, to bring about healing. Very likely when King Edward the Confessor of England initiated the mystique of the 'royal touch' for healing people, he was hypnotizing them, and the failure of the system generally in subsequent years might have been due to the fact that his successors did not have his technique.

Anton Mesmer (1734–1815) of Rudolfszell was a doctor who combined hypnotic techniques with a use of magnets. His cures were remarkable. He was a generous man (he commissioned Mozart to write *Bastien et Bastienne*) and treated poor people freely. His doctrine of the magnetic fluids may well have been related to the lines of vital force described in ACUPUNCTURE (*q.v.*). In spite of his countless cures, Mesmer was bitterly persecuted by the jealous medical profession.

Dr. John Elliotson, who hypnotized patients instead of filling their lungs with poisonous chemical anesthetics, was attacked by his medical colleagues who accused him of having bribed his patients not to scream while he operated! There are limits to what money can do, especially if your appendix is being cut out with a knife.

What then is hypnosis? Nobody knows. There are many conflicting opinions but nothing absolutely established other than the fact that it works. It is not sleep. Many people can be hypnotized and remain quite awake. In sleep people are not conscious of where they are, but a hypnotized person is. A hypnotic may resist and utterly reject ideas and suggestions made to him by the hypnotist, and break the spell. During sleep the heart and lungs show different patterns than are found during hypnosis, when the patterns are almost identical to those of a person awake.

If we look upon hypnotism as the surrender by one person to another of decision-making, control of the body, imagination, and the ability to concentrate, we shall not be far from the observable data.

Nobody can be hypnotized against his will, a point which Kipling demonstrated in *Kim*, and this is reassuring to many patients. Hypnosis is not a conditioned reflex, it is not due to fatigue in the nervous system, nor is it magic. The condition of a hypnotic is such that he or she responds favorably to most (not all) suggestions of the hypnotist, but usually forgets them afterwards.

There are various methods for inducing hypnotism, but a lot seems to depend upon the confidence and trust which the patient has in the hypnotist. Once the patient has been hypnotized, upon suggestions being made, he or she will feel no pain while an operation is being performed and can remember precisely and in exceptional detail events that happened forty years ago. There is, in cases of deep hypnosis, exceptional control over the muscles, and it has been known for a person to make his body as rigid as a plank between two separated chairs. It has also been shown that under hypnosis people are able to perform feats of greater strength than they otherwise can. Some have been induced to give up alcohol, smoking and drugs while under hypnosis. Self-confidence, ability in singing, speaking and lecturing have been improved by one or two sessions with a good, well-trained hypnotist. Enuresis (bed-wetting) and insomnia are often cured by hypnotism, as are many neurotic and psychosomatic illnesses. In some parts of the world it is used for painless childbirth, dentistry, high blood pressure and to control bleeding.

In spite of the appearance of hypnotists on stages and at fairs it is quite surprising that the orthodox medical professions throughout the world seem to have accepted hypnotism as a thoroughly respectable method of medical work. Admittedly the orthodox prefer to train their own operators, but that is all to the good, and it in no way excludes other people from learning hypnotism and using it for the good of their fellow human beings.

Owing to the facility with which a hypnotized person recalls detail, it is possible to use this method for careful diagnosis of conditions and unearth symptoms and details with great accuracy.

30

IONS FOR HEALTH

We are coming to learn that there is more to the envelope of air that supports life on this hospitable planet than its chemical constituents: nitrogen, oxygen and water vapor. Intense electrical activity takes place at the outer edge of the atmosphere where ultraviolet rays from the sun break down oxygen atoms, through a process called ionization, into negatively and positively charged particles which accumulate into a layer known as the ionosphere. Millions of years of ionization have produced a protective layer which now prevents damaging amounts of ultraviolet rays reaching the earth's surface and provides an electronic mirror which we use to bounce long-distance radio signals around corners on the earth's curvature.

Positively- and negatively-charged ions percolate down through the atmosphere to the earth's surface (they have a life of about a week) where they tend to be attracted by electrical polarization existing on the earth's surface. Thus, the bracing air of the seashore, the famous 'ozone', is no more than a concentration of negative ions in the atmosphere. Surf and waterfalls both increase the concentration of negative ions by prolonging their life and by adding new and more short-lived ions to the atmosphere.

A concentration of positive ions is detrimental to health. This condition is found in subterranean areas (underground railways, mines) and in the polluted conditions of urban living. Cigarette smoke and the cozy atmosphere of a crowd in a cinema or a cocktail party promote ion concentrations.

In those parts of France that are subjected to the sultry, warm mistral wind there is a curious accommodation made to the interpretation of the civil law. It is considered to be attenuating circumstances for a crime of passion!

Medical research has shown that an increased exposure of negative ions greatly speeds up the healing process. A number of hospitals now use this treatment for cases of severe burns.

Another intriguing practical application has been developed in Russia, where negative ionization equipment is now used in the Moscow underground system to offset the depressive effect of the concentration of positive ions.

Simple and effective equipment has been developed, and can be easily purchased for the individual to improve his local atmosphere. Models of ionizing equipment are made for use in a car (to counter the traffic-jam syndrome), in the home and in the office. They consume little electricity, and can be run off either batteries or mains supply.

As the therapeutic effect of these negative ion producers becomes more widely known, the equipment could become quite cheap. They counteract sleeplessness and depression, and seem to encourage well-being and the body's healing processes.

31.

JEWELS AS THERAPEUTIC AGENT

Diamonds are a girl's best friend, we are told. But for the more normal of us there may seem, at first sight, something almost pathological about the way ancient kings and rulers scrambled for jewels, hoarded them, and committed many crimes to get them. But there is a far more ancient tradition about jewelry than the one that connects it to beauty or fashion.

It is linked with the vibrations (as explained under RADIESTHESIA) and the influences which can be exerted with and through gems. Dr. Fernie nearly a century ago wrote a book about the curative properties he had discovered in jewels. It may be that this knowledge was absorbed from the Sanskrit writings and Indian traditions of the Aryan tribes many thousand years ago.

The jewels possess remarkably strong colors of the spectrum (see COLOR THERAPY). Applying royal blue gems to a burn is said to heal the burn and take away the pain, soothe exhausted nerves and tranquillize the patient. But there is one word of warning about using jewels as healing factors. They do not cease to irradiate their vibrations even when a patient has recovered from the indisposition, so they may throw something out of balance. Considerable knowledge and training is required to be able to handle them for therapy.

Gems are extremely powerful sources of color waves. Moreover, our experience should encourage us to open up this field of research. Apart from the work of a few great men, little has been done here for decades. For example, Dr. George Starr-White in his book *The Natural Way* wrote: 'Observation of insects and animals has shown that colour has a very specific effect upon them. Certain shades attract or repel, affecting the resistance to temperature and even pigmentation.'

The moonstone has a special link with Maya, mother of Gautama Buddha. It is held to refine and ennoble the soul of the person who wears it, to keep away influences that might detract from enlightenment.

How unscientific such writings seem. However, we should recall that the laser beam (light amplification by stimulated emission of radiation) can cut through the toughest metals like a Toledo blade through silk. It is used to perform the most intricate of eye surgery. How? Simply through using radiations in controlled form through a ruby!

32

KNEIPP'S WATER THERAPY

Sebastian Kneipp (1821–97) developed the use of water as a therapeutic much further than PRIESSNITZ (*q.v.*).

It seems incredible that this young student priest could develop such faith in God's goodness that he could attempt what no man before had recorded doing. Kneipp had a lung disease, considered in his day as fatal. He came across the work of Priessnitz' school. Instead of hiding away in bed with curtains drawn to keep out the sun (as the doctors recommended) he daily plunged his body into ice-cold water, and warmed himself with physical exercise. He became amazingly healthy and applied his experience to other sick people. Pastor Kneipp, whose methods brought health to millions when all other hopes had fled, became famous in Europe.

One of his recommendations was walking barefoot on wet grass or in a cold brook. He considered that walking on wet grass early in the morning was more effective than walking in a cold stream. The purpose is that the intense cold shall be followed by a resurgence of blood to the limbs, increasing their natural warmth. The legs are then dried, clad in warm hose, and exercised by a brisk walk. He also favored walking or running in freshly fallen snow, followed by a brisk drying massage and warm clothing. As a young man I always used to rub my body over with fresh snow whenever I got the chance. It is a magnificent tonic, and stops you feeling cold, provided that a quick rubdown with a rough towel follows.

Kneipp did not limit himself to the beneficial effects of cold water and other developments of Priessnitz' work. He developed a whole new school of therapy based upon water cures, light, fresh air and herbal teas.

In order to assess how effective Kneipp's work was, we have only to look at the fact that within his own lifetime, in spite of primitive, almost non-existent transport conditions, every year twenty thousand patients traveled to his little village of Wörishofen, and made it into a world-famous health resort.

Kneipp never succeeded in interesting the allopaths in his work. Evidence of countless cures was not enough; after all, he was only a priest without training, they reasoned; what could he know about healing the sick?

Germany, Austria and Switzerland remain the chief centers of the Kneipp cure.

33.

LAKHOVSKY'S OSCILLATORY COILS

In 1934 Georges Lakhovsky, a French engineer of Russian *émigré* extraction, propounded his theory of the oscillatory field. He produced a remarkable and complex instrument that could create an oscillatory field with therapeutic effects. The theory behind this is extremely advanced radiesthesia. The original apparatus was not only very large but extremely costly to make efficiently.

With transistors it has been possible to bring the equipment down to manageable size, and Dr. Bruce Copen has succeeded in doing so with a multiple wave oscillator consisting of two parts, one generative, the other resonant. The former creates activation of oscillatory circuits with considerable power of variation of frequencies controlled by dials and switches; the latter instrument resonates in harmony with the oscillatory frequencies produced by the generative instrument.

The patient sits between the two instruments and the oscillatory current passes through the living tissues of the patient, reactivating them to a correct, healthier vibratory pattern. Parts of the body or the entire body may be interposed into the path of the oscillatory current.

Dr. Copen, of Dane Hill, Sussex, has also discovered a method of transmitting an oscillatory current along the radionic wavelength of a patient who is not actually present, but mechanics of this operation are very advanced.

The Lakhovsky method has had exceptional results. I have myself taken part in experiments with the Copen equipment and found it very efficient.

Physiologists have shown that the human body is capable of broadcasting recognizable wave patterns that can modify atomic structures and build up organic compounds, that is, the protoplasm of life energy. Blood plasma, nerves and muscles are all capable of giving off rays. Dr. Gurwitsch (Leningrad) has recorded minute changes in wave patterns when carcinogenic changes build up in a healthy organism; the spectrum colors emitted in relationship to these emanations also change measurably, so that diagnosis of cancer in its earliest stages is possible by this method.

Lakhovsky did much research into sunspots as a source of radiations affecting plant growth, diseases and neuroses. He inoculated some plants with tumor-producing substances. When tumors had formed in them he placed short-wave oscillatory currents (about two meters) around one. This was the only plant that survived; the tumor fell off, leaving a clean scar. Scientists throughout the world repeated his experiments successfully. Andrevont and Shereshevsky of Harvard, two scientists who followed in the footsteps of Lakhovsky, demonstrated that the current destroyed cancerous growths in chickens and mice. Further confirmation was made by Dr. H. Ehrenwald (of the Vienna Neuropsychiatric Clinic) and by many other research scientists.

It is an acknowledged fact that in the nucleus of all known living cells there is an electrically oscillating twisted filament capable of transmitting and receiving radiations. Lakhovsky regarded disease as an oscillatory lack of equilibrium of the cells. He regarded the whole of creation as a seething conflict between radiations, not unlike Zoroaster's Ahura Mazda and Ahriman doctrine.

34

MIRACLE CURES

In *The Song of Bernadette*, Franz Werfel (1890–1945), the Austrian poet, wrote:

> For those who believe no explanation
> is necessary,
> For those who do not believe
> no explanation is possible.

When a scientist such as the Nobel prize-winner Alexis Carrel says in his book *L'Homme, L'Inconnu* that he has known miracles of healing to take place, it is difficult for lesser mortals to contradict. Alberto Denti de Pirajno in his *A Cure for Serpents*, Arthur Grimble in *A Pattern of Islands* and a large number of serious men have recorded miracles. I have known several miracles in my own life, but how does one begin to explain to somebody who was not there when it happened—above a fifteen-hundred-foot drop into an abyss, in an ocean storm, alone? I have visited Lourdes and Padua, among other shrines, where one may see tokens of thanksgiving offered by many who have been cured by miraculous healing.

Virtue does not seem to be the essential requisite for receiving a miracle. Sometimes compassion, love and foresight as to what a healed person may yet contribute to society may outweigh the personal worth, so that a miracle is granted. If you need one, pray for one.

Major McDermot, a frequent visitor to our family home, told us once of what had happened to him on Pitcairn Island, previously an intensely pious community. The islanders were suffering from a great economic crisis. The elders met and discussed the matter. They worked out that if they could catch one white whale their problems for the present would be solved. Our friend saw the entire island community gather and pray solemnly for one white whale. A couple of days later, one white whale swam into the bay and waited for the islanders to catch it. There had been no previous sign of any whales at all.

If you want a miracle, and you pray for one, make some sincere offer of something you will do if you get it, not as a bargain, but as an act of love and thanksgiving. An Italian friend of mine walked an enormous distance to pray at the shrine of a saint that his mother, who was desperately ill, might be spared to those that loved her. He could have taken a train, got a long-distance bus, cadged a lift, anything, but no. *'There was nothing I could think of doing for God,'* he explained, *'I had to show I was prepared to do something hard.'* I'm happy to say she recovered.

If you want life all your own way, getting and never giving, the chances of a miracle cure will be slimmer. Phrenosophists are perhaps the last religionists who believe unreservedly in miracles, but they say you have to live your life so as to make yourself worthy of consideration for a miracle.

35.

MUCOUS-FREE DIET THERAPY

This is, of course, an extension of DIETETICS (*q.v.*). It is based upon an attempt to free the mucous membrane of all impurities. Logically it is a fairly sound thesis.

The mucous membrane is, broadly speaking, the inside continuation of the skin which is outside our bodies. Imagine it folding back inside the mouth, and continuing right down throughout the body. Its thin lining covers all parts of the body which have any sort of access to the outside of the body. By this I refer to the lungs and respiratory system, to the mouth and the digestive system, and all parts connected with eating and drinking. It consists of several layers of tiny glands which produce a liquid secretion to keep the top layer mobile and fluid; this protects the surface from being injured by irritating substances and by hot foods. For people with a bad cold or constipation, hot food or hot drinks always produce an intensification of the stuffiness and discomfort that are symptomatic of their condition. This is because the work of the membrane has been rendered more difficult.

Substances such as APPLE CIDER VINEGAR (*q.v.*), orange juice, lemon and grapefruit juice (and these fruits eaten whole) do much to tone up the membranes. Carbohydrate foods do not; curries, pickles, sauces, mayonnaises, foods with artificial chemicals and the like all clog up the membranes.

One of the reasons why it is helpful to chew raw onions (cut them once or twice if you have a small mouth and a big onion), or cloves of garlic, or leeks, is because these vegetables have a remarkable scouring effect upon the mucous membranes. I once cured a very severe and stubborn case of Vincent's angina with a course of chewing two or three cloves of garlic every hour for a six-hour period. Nothing else had succeeded in ridding the patient of this painful throat condition. Of course, chewing onions and raw cloves of garlic is unpleasant. Garlic has a burning, bitter taste which is only possible to endure because of the knowledge of its curative effect.

Some people find that a mild stomach upset occurs as a result of eating garlic. Generally this clears up within twenty-four hours, but if it persists, make some leek soup using fresh milk, and take that for a day instead. One teaspoonful of slippery elm (*Ulmus fulva*), taken upon rising with an equal portion of honey and a cupful of warm (not boiled) milk, is a very mild but very efficient way of clearing the mucous membrane. This should be taken before breakfast and again after supper; three days should produce very satisfactory results.

Avoid purgatives and laxatives, cocoa, chocolate, coffee and strong tea other than nourishing herbal teas.

36

MUSIC AS THERAPY

When Dame Sybil Thorndike, one of the world's greatest actresses, was asked how she felt about music, she replied: 'After God—Bach!' Her earliest ambition was to become a pianist, but it was otherwise decreed.

The ancient Greeks were among the first recorded people to realize the importance of music in daily life. Gymnastics and many work tasks were all performed to music. Plato expressed his concept thus: 'As gymnastics to the body, so is music necessary for the health of the soul.' 'If music be the food of love, play on', exclaims Duke Orsino in Shakespeare's *Twelfth Night*. In fact it is possible for music to be a stimulant or antidote to almost any human emotion. Theodor T. Munger called music 'the vehicle of emotion and thought.'

One thinks of the piety and spiritual aspirations conveyed by Vivaldi's *Gloria,* the old carol *In Dulci Jubilo,* or Byrd's *Ave Verum* which is for me a remarkably spiritual piece of composing. Young people often find bliss in Tchaikowsky's *Romeo and Juliet, Francesca da Rimini, Swan Lake,* etc.

I remember how John Gough, the Australian composer, told me of how much research and work had gone into his *Corroboree,* which contains more earthy primitive feelings than Stravinsky's *Rite of Spring*.

In my time I have listened to Ute and Sioux chants, shamanistic Lapp *Joïk,* the inspired compositions (sung by himself) of Salvatore Adamo (Belgium's great pop star), Edith Piaf, the one and only Amalia Rodrigues, poetess of the *Fado,* the crystal-voiced Katri Helena of Helsinki, the shanties of the *Nordermeyer Heimatverein*. But when I seek more profound emotional responses I go to Sibelius, Bach's *Goldberg Variations* or Beethoven.

To get the full therapeutic effects from music one must

explore it. One must recognize differences in the depth of
emotions. There are occasions when the sparkle and vivacity
of the final aria in Rossini's *Cenerentola,* a chanson of Fauré,
or Schubert *Lieder,* will not provide the answer that Gilbert
and Sullivan's tripping melodies or Lehar's *Merry Widow* will
offer. (The latter was Hitler's great favorite.)

I met Svetlana Beriosova, the Lithuanian-born ballerina, on
the occasion of her first London triumph. 'Music has its own
feeling for me,' she said. This is the secret of using music for
therapeutical purposes; it is basically an individual therapy.

Mystics used to ring bells to drive away evil spirits, and
much music may come from the use of sonic vibrations for
magic incantations. One has only to hear the rhythms of Bali
or Africa to recognize the transmission of vibrations. The
Lapps used a specially made drum of reindeer skin for magic
purposes; there is an uncanniness in the effectiveness of their
magic.

With regard to vocal music, much depends upon the rapport between the singer's personality and the mood of the
composer. I remember one singularly brilliant singer being
criticized for singing the role of *Carmen* like a country vicar's
daughter, whereas Prosper Mérimée's exasperating gypsy in
Bizet's opera is no lady, rather a gutter slut with violent pas-
sions and a total disregard for consequences.

Nobody ever sang Wagnerian *Götterdammerung* parts like
Kirsten Flagstad, but we should remember that the resurgence of primitive Aryan religious ideas at that time gave
more meaning and background for the singer to draw upon.

We must not forget the importance of RADIESTHESIA
(*q.v.*) in explaining vibrations to us. A sick person has distinctly something wrong with his vibrational pattern. Although it may seem difficult to comprehend, we must bear in
mind that if cows can give better milk yields when listening to
soothing music (such as Strauss waltzes), it is not unrea-
sonable to expect a change of mood for sick humans.

When it is autumn next, listen to the *Automne* of Cécile
Chaminade (Paris, 1857–1944), one of Bizet's favorite
composers. My mother loved her works, for Chaminade was
an accomplished pianist. One of my most harrowing and
unhappy love affairs as a young man was greatly helped by

playing until the record nearly wore out Fischer-Dieskau's recital of Beethoven's song cycle *An die ferne Geliebte:*

> *Dann vor diesen Liedern weichet*
> *Was geschieden uns so weit,*
> *Und ein liebend Herz erreichet,*
> *Was ein liebend Herz geweiht.*

Another approach to the therapeutic side of music is learning to play an instrument yourself. It is a painstaking effort, unless you only play the cymbal, but such a remarkable method of self-expression that it provides a tremendous outlet for emotional feelings and problems. I cannot repeat too often the need to explore all branches of music. Too many young people explore only the rhythmic beat of their contemporary pop heroes. They could find more solutions to their problems by widening the range of their musical adventures and explorations. There are no new problems, only new inexperienced human beings.

It is very remarkable that the staid, allopathic branch of healing has come to recognize that in many cases music has a beneficial effect upon patients. Some of the earliest work was done at Horton Hospital, Epsom, Surrey, a large mental home. Many patients have found their first steps to recovery by listening to concerts. Music breaks down the nervous tensions, helps them to forget shock memories that have been intruding into their everyday waking life.

At Cambridge, Massachusetts, a dentist recorded that he had extracted hundreds of teeth and conducted thousands of fillings, using music only and no drug or anesthetics. In Boston, surgeons have delivered babies, excised cysts, and they say they have even probed the heart of a patient using soothing music and no anesthetic. In confirmation of the therapeutic property of music, some medical men of the University of Michigan have established to their satisfaction that harp music relieves patients who have hysterical symptoms and that violin solos take away migraines and headaches.

It is surmised that the area of the brain, first discovered by Dr. Gall, through which music is expressed and registered blocks off the sensations of pain and discomfort. This would seem a mental counterpart of ACUPUNCTURE (*q.v.*).

37.

NATURE CURE

What has come to be known as Nature Cure is basically a combination of fasts (Guelphe, Schroth, etc.) and strict attention to DIETETICS (*q.v.*). The basic idea behind all variations of Nature Cure is that the body can and will heal itself if not damaged with drugs whose side effects are largely unknown.

Harry Benjamin's *Everybody's Guide to Nature Cure* has remained a great classic on the subject for forty years. Nature Cure is a very broad philosophy, and like the Hindu religion in which one may be monotheistic or polytheistic, the label hides a wide variety of emphases. The Nature Cure establishments that have flourished increasingly in the last fifty years adhere to different theories, some preferring one type of fast, some another; occasionally (especially in Germany) baths and sun treatment are favored. One thing most of the establishments have in common, apart from the broad general principles of dietetics and fasting, is a good record for cures and healthy patients. It has been said that Nature Cure homes force people to follow the diets for which they lack the will to apply themselves without aid. This is a misrepresentation. There is a group-therapy effect of patients being together and able to enjoy a social life.

Some homes are more expensive than others, but then the foods are not those of the mass shopping supermarkets. For example, bread, which is stone-ground, baked according to old recipes and prepared without any chemicals, is much more expensive (as well as being more healthy).

In Germany much of the original thinking about Nature Cure was done by Kneipp, Rikl, Schroth and Kuhn, who did research into vitamins. In America, Stanley Lief, Gayelord Hauser and others have carried on the crusade which Jackson, Kellogg, Lindlahr, Tilden and Trall initiated. It is interesting that the old phrenologists were some of the earliest advocates of food reform.

Both biochemics and homeopathy are on the fringe of Nature Cure. Herbalism is nearer, for what could be more natural than the use of herbs as dietetic aids?

38.

NEGATIVE GREEN THERAPY

The discovery of this force was made by an Egyptian in 1942. He was doing some research on the radiations of the pyramids when he experienced radiations which were unlike any previously encountered. When the pendulum was tuned for the color green it began to rotate in a negative direction instead of positive.

The scope of this force is enormous. The radiation field within the Great Pyramid of Cheops is such that some people faint or feel ill if they get the full blast of its vibrations. May be it was this same force in the stone that Colonel Fawcett had, and which lured him back to the lost jungles of Brazil, from which he never returned alive. (A psychometrist had told him that the stone had originated in the lost continent of Atlantis.)

Harnessed and used in correct proportion, the vibrations give a radiation field which has shown itself to be therapeutic.

A further discovery along this path of research showed some peculiar sand which revealed pyramidal shapes under microscopic examination. This sand, which is not green in color, is extremely fine in texture and has the quality of transmitting what has come to be called negative green among advanced radiesthesists. Used in small quantities, from a drachm to an ounce, it has shown distinct therapeutic properties. One unusual claim made for it is that it can protect the human aura from influences upsetting the correct balance. Many claims for its beneficial workings have been made, but most of them are more within the occult field than the purely therapeutic.

39.

OCCUPATIONAL THERAPY

'I haven't got time to be ill,' my mother often said, 'I'm too busy.' Many decades later I recognized the essence of wisdom of her words. Her love and her interests were too all-embracing: the family, the cats, music, her physical exercises.

We are all used to hearing about the puppet-making, crochet work and similar occupations which keep hospital patients' minds away from their conditions. Few people know that the idea was first propounded by Dr. J. G. Spurzheim, M.D., L.C.P. (London), and of the universities of Vienna and Paris, in his book *Observation on the Deranged Manifestations of the Mind*.[1] He was, with Gall, one of the founders of phrenology. The idea was developed by George Combe, lawyer and phrenologist of Edinburgh, and passed into common acceptance.

A busy person may become ill, but generally less seriously than a person whose time is idled away with no great interests, other than listening to pop music, etc.

A sick person may find great relief in reading, in planning a new idea, a new venture. It may easily take over and become a sound motive for recovery. When I was very ill indeed with tuberculosis of the lungs, my Canadian cousin, the poet Larry Rowdon, spoke to me a lot about an expedition we could make together into Northern Canada; he even kidded

[1] Boston, Mass., 1833.

me into learning some phrases of Indian languages, Eskimo
customs and much else. We never did make that trip, but
planning it got me over a very difficult patch. I refused all
medication and was cured by bed rest, vitamins, the mercy of
God and the prayers of those who loved me. Within a year or
two I was sleeping out rough on damp ground, climbing
mountains, doing weightlifting, swimming, running and
much else. Everybody I knew at the sanatorium who had had
the allopathic medical cure remained an invalid for life, and
never did any of those things. One thing a sick person can do
is to try to write something, to draw, to paint, to create something good. When you are doing something positive your vibrations turn away from the negative (sick) side of life.
Sickness is often a turning-point in a person's life, a time for
reflection and change during which he matures into a positive,
powerful creative personality. Even sickness can be made into
an opportunity to succeed.

40.

OSTEOPATHY

Andrew T. Still (1828–1917) was the founder of the system of healing known as osteopathy. His father was a Methodist minister and doctor to his parish. The family followed
the peregrinations of the minister's appointments, including
trek by covered prairie schooner, lasting many weeks, from
eastern Tennessee to Missouri. It is believed that Still first
went to medical school at the age of eighteen. He became a
qualified doctor of medicine, which took the wind out of the
sails of his opponents. Andrew Still was an extremely intelligent man who mastered fluency in the Shawnee language at
an early age.[1] He was a man for whom humanity mattered

[1] Owing to its grammatical complexity this was an exceptional
intellectual feat.

more than issues; at great risk to himself he deliberately fed
Confederate troops although himself enrolled in the Federal
army.

In 1864 Still met one of those great trials in life which so
often mark the careers of great men. All three of his children
died of meningitis. None of his skill and training as a doctor
could save them; his disillusionment with 'orthodox' medicine
was total. His Methodist background consoled him. He per-
ceived that God is a God of perfection, and that, as a creation of God's, man must contain perfectibility and have been
planned upon a perfect design. (This echoes the teaching of
George Combe, the phrenologist, who lectured extensively in
America a quarter of a century earlier.)

Still reasoned that, directly or otherwise, man must induce
deviations from the plan of perfection himself. The logical
step beyond this was that God has provided answers to help
man achieve healing; that the body has within itself the power
to heal, as Hippocrates had said two millenniums previously.
Still began to study, with exceptional precision and powers of
observation, the anatomy of man and animals in detail. He
discovered methods of diagnosis which had escaped less profound thinkers than himself. He found that he could diagnose
conditions by touching areas of the body to judge the speed
of, heat of and quality of blood palpitating beneath the area;
this was called palpation. It is akin to natural RADIESTHESIA
(q.v.) and bears some relationship to the theory of vital
force channels referred to by ACUPUNCTURISTS.

His researches bore not only fruit but a bounteous harvest.
Not only did he demonstrate that many illnesses have a relationship to disorders of the spine, and could be reversed by
manipulating joints back into correct alignment, but also that
sicknesses such as erysipelas and many types of respiratory
ailments could be healed by his methods. *The whole tenor of
Still's researches emphasised the way in which illness is related to a condition of the whole body and is not an isolated
outbreak in just one part of it.*

Still's methods were revolutionary because he looked beyond the symptoms of his patients and painstakingly traced
the sickness to a cause. He demonstrated in front of officials
and doctors of the state of Missouri, to their amazement and

admiration, setting dislocations which many of them had found impossible, even with a patient under anesthetic. Reading about osteopathy, however, is like reading about tying knots and splices without a piece of string in your hands. He is said also to have cured patients of epilepsy and gallstones, as well as some cases of cancer and tuberculosis.

The advantages of Still's methods are that the cure is virtually instantaneous. When the cause is removed, the conditions set up by the cause disappear fairly quickly afterwards. The disadvantage, if one can call it that, is that Still was an exceptional man, and not all, though certainly many, of his pupils could achieve his brilliant touch. However, sufficient people were interested enough to establish the American School of Osteopathy which Still founded, and which began as a small clapboard, traditional American building and is now an even more typical American massively imposing edifice in Kirksville, Missouri.

Allopaths claim to be able to cure everything, but osteopaths are aware of certain limits, such as that vitamin and mineral salt deficiencies are often behind the loss of muscular tone and the consequent falling out of alignment of bones. If such deficiencies are not made good, the bones will easily fall out of position again if realigned. Osteopathy does offer us bloodless surgery. Certain arthritic conditions, the slipped disc, asthmatic-bronchitic conditions which can be due to lesions of the spine behind the shoulder blades, muscular atrophy, the back pains that are common to women, the Parkinson syndrome, pneumonia, to say nothing of practically every form of dislocation known have all yielded to the magic touch of trained osteopaths.

Modern osteopaths work with X rays to examine the position of the joints, paying especial attention to spinal lesions which, it is known, influence the entire body by the pressure they place upon the nervous system and the blood vessels.

The theory of osteopathy is supported historically by the insistence of the ancient Greeks upon physical exercises and gymnastics, not only for the young but for those of all ages; very little those wise forefathers did was purely for idle amusement, however pleasurable it was in execution. The old Roman saw *'Mens sana in corpore sano'* came to life anew in

Still's dictum that unless the structure of the body is healthy its working cannot be healthy. He went so far as to declare that where blood is circulating normally disease cannot develop, since he reasoned that blood can defeat disease. But as dietitians would hasten to explain, this means pure, perfect blood, devoid of artificial chemicals, toxic substances, DDT, chlorinated hydrocarbons, mercury, etc.

Still constantly referred to the fluids of life, by which the lymphatic system is included as well as the blood. He seems also to have intended within the definition forces which are described by Reichenbach, Lakhovsky and others, whose approach borders more upon the field of radiesthesia than physiology. The inability to understand the potential of such fluid forces is one reason why people with a purely materialistic medical training cannot just pick up a textbook on osteopathy and make it work with the same facility of a do-it-yourself build-a-dinghy book.

Still was opposed to alcoholic drinks and to any substances which induced the autointoxication of the body; he thought (as James Hilton was to echo later in his novel *Lost Horizon*) that most people commit suicide because of their stresses and tensions and the autointoxication these set up.

One group of osteopaths, overwhelmed by the blandishments of recognition, professional status, equal privileges, etc., decided to ally itself to the established medical body, the allopaths, in the state of California. Unfortunately for them there was one little clause in the bond which was possibly inserted with a *Shylock* insouciance, since it demanded worse than a pound of flesh from the victims: they were to handle only patients recommended by the allopathic doctors. This sounded fine until it turned out that the allopaths were sending few patients to their new allies. As Bugs Bunny might put it, 'With friends like that, who needs enemies?'

This sad experience is good advice to all practitioners of the alternative healing arts. Or, as Kipling expressed the warning:

> One watchword through our Armies
> One answer from our lands:—
> 'No dealings with Diabolus
> As long as Man's soul stands.'

41

PHRENOLOGY

This is a much neglected system of analyzing character and the human Mind. It has been vulgarly dismissed by the medical profession and others as reading the bumps on the head, in spite of the fact that average heads do not have any bumps at all.

Just as a gymnast or athlete develops certain muscles in preference to others according to the type of activity he goes in for, there is, say phrenologists, a distinct relationship in some parts of the brain to the activity of certain faculties of the Mind. Latter-day phrenologists, calling themselves phrenoanalysts, state categorically that the Mind operates the body through the brain. The word 'Mind' with a capital letter indicates the entire spiritual personality of the being.

Phrenology provides a unique method of diagnosing illnesses. In fact, phrenologists were about a century ahead of the foundation of the psychosomatic school of thought. The theory was the linking of unhealthy mental activity of certain characteristics with nervous, muscular and general weaknesses, tendencies to sickness, etc.

It generally takes about two to three years to learn the system of analysis properly. Allowances must be made for time to learn about the frontal sinus, hair growth and other difficulties in the way of a beginner taking up the charts and practicing.

The position of the areas on the external surface of the skull is oblique in relationship to the corresponding areas on the surface of the brain. All parts of the brain are multipurpose, which does not make it easier to understand phrenology, though admittedly making it more fascinating. The shapes of the areas vary according to the shape of the skull, so that a long-headed person will not have the same shaped areas as a brachycephalic person, or the rarer scaphoid.

One of their tenets is that the development of any mental faculty over a certain degree is most likely to unbalance the entire personality. Thus, most of them would classify nine stages of development in each area; the middle five degrees were safe, but the two lowest and the two largest degrees were likely to bring imbalance, and result in physical ill health as well as neurotic behavior. Over five thousand books have been written upon the subject in some thirty languages, but the system, however effective, is hard to study, and even successful students have had little thanks and much ridicule and persecution to expect. The Italian authorities persecuted Professor Uccelli and his family so much that he committed suicide. In the brutal, organized attacks on phrenology it has been overlooked that it embodied the philosophical work of Auguste Comte and Herbert Spencer.

The system was founded by F. J. Gall (1756–1828), who was one of the most successful physicians of Vienna and Paris, attending court and embassy patients. Unlike some modern research workers who publish their findings after a year or two, Gall took over thirty leisurely years to produce massive, fully detailed volumes with engravings so perfect that they rival modern photographs of the brain. He excelled in so many fields (psychology, criminology, sociology, etc.) that it would be difficult to list them all. He wrote the *Introduction au Cours de Physiologie du Cerveau, Recherches sur le Système Nerveux, Anatomie et Physiologie du Système Nerveux*, etc. He was joined by another doctor of merit, J. G. Spurzheim, whose works included *The Physiognomical System of Drs. Gall & Spurzheim*. He saw better than Gall the uses to which the discoveries of Gall could be put. The less well-known George Combe, a brilliant Edinburgh lawyer, wrote *The Constitution of Man*, which was at one time second only to the Bible in its sales figures, remarkable for a relatively devout age. This was the first, positive, coherent compilation of the philosophy of phrenology.

The phrenologists had an uncanny knack of telling the truth quite regardless of consequences. They upset Napoleon, who ordered the Académie Française to find against them.

They upset the royal family because of their criticisms of the head of Edward VII. They made unfashionable statements such as that a person born with a naturally brilliant intellect should be trained as a doctor or a diplomat even if he were the son of a dustman; that a man who was the son of a duke but an absolutely no-good scoundrel had better become a roadsweeper. Since speaking the truth was a matter of honor and courage, phrenologists' public relations image was bad.

In the field of analysis the phrenologists were more successful in technique than in organization. There were at one time 136 societies for phrenology in Britain; phrenoanalysis is only taught, in modernized form, by the phrenosophists, and they are generally unwilling to teach anybody who is not of their religion. It is one of those subjects that nobody could learn in a century without help from an expert. Lack of support precluded the phrenologists from establishing a unified training college.

Among the most famous phrenologists were Joseph Millott-Severn, his wife and Stackpoole O'Dell and his family, who established an unequaled record for brilliance of technique, accuracy and sincerity, creating a legend that finished only with the death of the great Millott-Severn in 1942. Stackpoole O'Dell and Millott-Severn both wrote philosophical essays upon the more profound aspects of phrenology.

42.

PHRENOSOPHICAL
SPIRITUAL HEALING

This is a unique form of healing because the healer sits in meditation, asking for divine guidance about the patient. The guidance comes in the form of advice about which of a number of different colored silk cords to select, and how many of each color to take. These are then woven by the healer into a length such as will go around the patient's wrist or over the place of the hurt or pain. (They are never worn around the neck.)

A phrenosophical service takes place and the silken cords are blessed by the healer. From that moment on the cords are not allowed to be touched by anybody except the patient; even the healer handles them with tongs; the patient must never allow anybody to touch them except himself/herself.

The system is a blend of spiritual healing, color therapy and radiesthesia. It has been known to work some exceptional cures. There is only one difficulty. Phrenosophists dislike publicity, and unless you know one, the chances of finding one are remote.

43.

PHYSICAL CULTURE AS THERAPY

The ancient Greeks encouraged physical culture, gymnastics and sport among people of all ages.

I remember how surprised I was to learn that a man I saw regularly at the swimming baths was seventy years old. Every day after a brisk swim of 400 meters he would stand on the side and do some physical exercises immediately after the shower and before drying himself. He had a physique that many young men of twenty would have aspired to. Nor had anybody known him to have had a day's illness.

We must all grow old. It is the first price for living in our bodies (the second is dying), but how we grow old makes all the difference. Why let the body become full of aches, pains and stiff joints? Why become so 'busy' that we can never make time to do a few minutes' exercise every day?

Man was built to move; movement is life, and without movement life becomes more a way of dying.

Exercise invigorates the body, drives the blood with its oxygen and mineral salts, etc., on its way, forces the secretions of our glands into the remote tissues where they are needed, prevents constipation, and keeps the heart fit. Furthermore it opens up the body's alveolar cells to the life-giving oxygen without which nothing can operate properly. Regular exercise establishes a self-discipline which can come in handy in all fields of human activity.

Many cases of obesity, catarrh, rheumatic and other conditions could be reversed at an early stage if only people would make time for a short, regular run in a track suit around the block, ten minutes' exercise with a 'Bullworker' or similar muscle-tension apparatus, or perhaps a short workout with weights (light weights, low repetitions and quick movements tone up the system very well). Too much alcohol, too many short nights without sleep, too much smoky, polluted air, all damage man's health, eroding away vitality.

A physically fit body will be its own judge of diet. The fitter you are the easier it is to assess what foods you require and how much.

Free-standing exercises without any weights or instruments can be performed in the smallest of rooms or apartments, but do not try to overdo the effort if you are just starting after many years not exercising, or for the first time. There are plenty of excellent books to help a beginner, and remember it is better to do five minutes every day than an hour once a week. Social sports and games are good for you but do not have the same therapeutic effect that exercises have.

44

PHYSIOTHERAPY

by T. J. H. N. Law, F.Phys.I., M.S.M.A., A.S.Chir.

This is a modern, descriptive word for the art of massage. The operator (masseur or masseuse) compels the body to act as it normally should by its own efforts. Conditions of ill health often mean that the bodily functions are unable to be carried on by the body of its own volition. When, for example, a limb has been broken or fractured, it will not be used properly and therefore it cannot draw the normal amount of nutrients from the body's supply of 'fuel,' let alone the extra required to restore it to full health and working order.

'Fuel' in this context means the materials that the human body is able to manufacture to keep itself healthy, as when a foreign body enters the skin through a perforation, the white leucocytes immediately fly to that area. A perfectly healthy body is one in which all parts are working without friction or irritation. Each part, however small, requires and should get the necessary nutrients which it requires to function. If the part is not worked it does not draw to itself the nutrients, which is why some yogis who hold their arms out stiff by sheer will power for months and years find the arms wither completely and never return to normal use. No work—no fuel! If one part is not worked it may also starve another part which is dependent upon the first; this sets up trouble and irritation which may have far-reaching effects stretching throughout the body to distant parts. One of the difficulties of massage is learning to work 'backwards' to effect a cure, but treatment of the original cause is always more positive in its results, and quicker to heal the patient's discomfort and pain.

The message of massage is that by helping the body to do

its natural work, after correct diagnosis of the trouble, restoration occurs more quickly and safely.

I know of a case where a doctor asked a masseur to call on a patient whom the doctor said had sciatica. The masseur, who always made his own diagnosis, examined the patient, and told her that if he were to treat the sciatica to relieve the pain he would have to call three times a day, which would be expensive and time consuming. He referred back to the doctor, and asked him to agree to his treating another condition that was the basic cause of the sciatica. The doctor consented. The masseur said the results should show up by the third session, and the doctor agreed to call and examine the patient. The masseur's diagnosis proved correct and produced excellent results. The cause was removed, and within a short time the patient, who had been bedridden and in great pain for two years, was completely cured. Massage had achieved what years of drugs had failed to do. This is not an indictment of the doctor, who had merely followed the traditions of his training, but it does show that massage has a lot to offer.

There is in healing an element of vibrations, and this enters into massage (see RADIESTHESIA). When the masseur works upon an injured limb he helps it to return to the correct vibrational pattern which is associated with normalcy of functioning. Just as if one part of a computer is not functioning properly it can have effects upon the efficiency of the entire machine, so if part of the body is not functioning it affects all of the body, more or less. The process of healing is speeded up if the operator can attune himself to the patient, establishing a rapport on a harmonious wavelength. The more sensitive the masseur is to the patient, the better his understanding of the condition, the better the response of the patient to the ministrations provided to heal him.

In the case of a fracture or break in the limb, adjacent parts, not the actual area, are massaged lightly to help the condition. As a condition begins to mend, the massage can be followed by light exercise.

One aspect of massage which is mystifying to many patients is that much of the pressure is very light, and effected by the fingers; rarely is it necessary for heavy, powerful pressure to be exerted. This emphasizes what I have said about the vibratory effects of massage. The result is improvement in the circulation of the blood, and spreading the distribution of oxygen to tissues and cells. Massage causes the rapid absorption of waste products in the muscles, and improves the circulation of lymph.

The movements are classified as *effleurage*, or stroking, in which the hand is moved in one direction only; *petrissage*, or kneading, consisting of rolling, squeezing and rubbing with some pressure exerted by fingers or knuckles or, more generally, with the ball of the thumb; *tapotement*, a vibratory movement. There are also movements such as thrusting, hacking, and passive limb movement which is very useful for stiff joints.

Among conditions which massage can help are neuralgia, neuritis, rheumatic and sciatic conditions, Bell's paralysis, hysteria, St. Vitus's dance and a very wide range of muscular disabilities. Constipation and some obesity cases also yield very well to massage.

45.

PRIESSNITZ WATER CURES

Vicenz Priessnitz (1799–1851) was one of those giant figures whose deeds raise them above their fellows for intelligence, steadfastness of purpose and for the beneficial results of their life work. When this simple untutored Silesian farmer professed to cure people through the use of cold water the medical profession divided only between those that ridiculed him to scorn and others who wept tears of laughter at his expense. 'Truth is the only daughter of Time,' declared Leonardo da Vinci; those who laughed last laughed best. Priessnitz had discovered something that had escaped the high and mighty, and, as it is written in the *Magnificat*, God exalted the humble and the meek yet once more. Priessnitz' exceptional successes led to the establishment of a cold-water-cure resort on the Gräfenberg, and many have followed since then.

The Cheyenne tribe, before missionaries taught them it was 'wicked' to bathe and walk around naked, dipped into a freezingly cold river winter and summer alike every morning upon rising. Until they gave up this habit they had exceptionally good health.

Bacteria seem to dislike the cold much more than the heat, for it renders the conditions in which they could breed easily most unsuitable. Professor Malinowski (if my memory serves me correctly) did some of the first experiments in cold and almost absolute zero (magnetically induced) and demonstrated that cold rather than heat may be the chief generator of life-forming energy. Mercury will climb the sides of a container, and move like an intelligent animal to get to a lower surface than that of the magnetically induced almost absolute zero! Here again is a field of research which needed study but has been comparatively neglected.

Here is one of the Priessnitz treatments which is still followed fairly widely on the Continent. It is called the winding. First, a wet towel is wound around the naked patient. Round this a layer of nettles is laid. Then there follows a thick blanket which keeps the water against the patient. Treatments like these are given to patients resting in bed. Honey-sweetened herbal teas are served frequently, and the feet and hands are kept warm. The patient must have evacuated the bowel and bladder first. The windings are usually changed every hour. Temperature readings are taken every thirty minutes to stop the patient becoming too cold. Warm windings are given for fevers, and changed every half hour. The treatment should only be applied by somebody properly trained in Priessnitz' methods.

Oak bark was often used in the windings for weeping eczema; camomile flowers for wounds that did not heal well, inflammations, etc.; calamus for circulatory troubles of arms, legs, etc.; oat straw for rheumatic ills and chills.

See KNEIPP, SAUNA.

46.

PSYCHOMETRY

I have heard allopathic doctors scoff at spiritualism and condemn it as 'stuff and nonsense'. I would, however, like to tell the truth and shame the devil as the old evangelists used to say, and I am glad to set forth the following facts.

Some spiritualist mediums are possessed of a remarkable talent which became known during the last century as psychometry. I have been present at meetings where a spiritualist medium has been handed an object belonging to a person who was totally unknown to the medium, and who was not even present in the room. The psychometrist (often a woman) would close her eyes, hold the object carefully, and begin to speak. The sex, age, physical description of the person, color of hair, eyes, shape of features (for instance, a short nose) would be given in exact detail. Sometimes a psychometrist would say such things as this: the person I am describing has had a bad fall during her teens, the hip was injured but it mended, the healing was not completed, there is still pain there, the spine has been jolted and never put right; or, the person to whom this belongs has had a long history of liver trouble, he suffers from a lot of pain, there is a stone forming in his bladder. Often advice would be given too.

I have never known a psychometrist be wrong, provided the specimen given was unadulterated. Theirs is a natural radiesthetic sense on a very high spiritual plane. As a method of diagnosis it is exceptionally valuable, but of course, many highly qualified allopaths who have never attended a séance in their lives will no doubt assure us that it is all an illusion. Maybe, but does it matter if it works efficiently? Most of these gifted persons would work entirely without payment, because they felt that if they made a living out of it the psychic gift would disappear and never return.

There are some spiritualists in nearly all the great centers of world civilization, and it should not be too difficult to find through them somebody who has the gift of psychometry. Its possession depends rather upon the state of spiritual enlightenment, and it cannot be crammed at any study course in a couple of semesters.

47.

PSYCHOSOMATIC HEALING

The relationship of mind and body is very closely interwoven. The natural capacities of human beings in a difficult situation are two, fight or flight, applied either physically or mentally, in various combinations.

Human beings have more complicated thought processes than any animal. Mental phenomena such as self-respect, frustrated friendship, snubs, conflict of loyalties, unhappiness (*Weltschmerz*), or feelings of inadequacy, all produce situations that provide confusion between fight and flight. One could punch the boss on the nose, walk out, set fire to the building and so on, but these are so primitive and irresponsible (and not without retribution) that the chance to do something is often repressed into a miserable mumble.

Nor can most urban dwellers pack their bags and flee to the depths of the forests or to some sun-kissed tropical island. There are the mortgage payments, the installments on the TV set, on the car, on the freezer, and a thousand and one commitments, all and each of which add up to making a difficult life a bit more comfortable.

Very often disappointments, hurts, frustrations and violent emotions are then turned inward toward the body and its delicate functions. Anger and frustration can, if strong enough in feeling, change the chemical constitution of the stomach acids within a couple of minutes! The blood, the lymphatic secretions of the body are at the mercy of the mind, and from their behavior the muscles and even the bones take their health, or ill health.

Dr. Flanders Dunbar was one of the world's greatest authorities on psychosomatic medicine. Her research, and that of equally brilliant colleagues, showed how emotional behavior could lead to constant tensing of the muscles, and this to fibrositis, rheumatic and arthritic complaints. Insecurity, or the feeling of having let oneself down, can induce angina pectoris, migraine, asthma and coronary thrombosis; how many middle-aged and older men feel they have failed in their lives, and suffer a stroke!

It is known that two people may have the same disease with identical symptoms, and one get better, the other pass away. This, say the followers of psychosomatic medicine, shows how the human mind can influence the body.

People who can never cope with their social and personal lives are always likely to get ill. Any fool can kid himself he can change human nature and society (whatever that means) and solve the problems of the world by the methods of Genghis Khan or Al Capone, but he is only delaying his own maturity—and that of others. The American Indians kept fit hunting down the buffalo; when the herds were extinguished they sickened and died too. *Difficulties are the measure of man. Every problem solved brings its own glory, and the more we succeed, the better equipped we become to succeed further.* People who are frequently sick should study this approach to healing.

48

RADIESTHESIA AND RADIONICS

In order to present the outlines of this complicated and enormous field of study concisely, it is impossible to detail more than a sketch of the methods of proof.

If some of the details of radiesthesia and its electronic, computerized form, radionics, seem fantastic, I beg the reader to act upon the ancient Greek proverb, which wisely instructs us not to give a verdict until we have heard both sides of the argument.

We are now accustomed to the orbiting man-made satellites that can detect changes in the weather days before they occur where we live, and heat rays many miles above the earth's crust. We appreciate the homing device by which a surface-to-air missile may pick up at great distances the heat waves emitted by an aircraft, beam onto them and hit it.

The work of Wilhelm Conrad von Röntgen (1845–1923) in demonstrating the existence of X rays (for which he won the Nobel Prize for Physics in 1901) showed us that totally invisible rays could pass through the human body and produce a shadow picture of the human skeleton and tissues, organs, etc., upon a sensitized plate.

In most homes there is a record player, on which records are played. On these, varying forms are used in a continuous, circular line to reproduce vibrations in the frequencies of sound. A transistor radio selects according to tuning specific frequencies, picks up waves of transmitted vibrations and converts them into recognizable signals.

Ultrasonics is a term used for vibrations of density in the air (or similar elastic media) which exceed 20,000 cycles per second, and many reach 10,000,000 cycles per second. Scientists make use of these for such varied ends as brain sur-

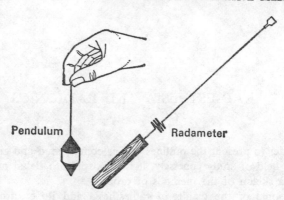

Pendulum · Radameter

RADIESTHESIA INSTRUMENTS

gery and sounding the depth of the ocean. Bats and some other nocturnal animals use ultrasonics to guide their movements in the dark. From them man learned to use radar, by which ultrasonic beams are transmitted, hit an object, bounce back and give us the distance and other data about the object they have returned from. The interesting thing is that radar has always existed. Bats are some of the oldest mammals in creation. In my *Young Person's Nature Guide* I told the story of the old Abbé Spallanzani's experiment which demonstrated that bats could find their way in a darkened room through a crisscross of strings in it. Radiesthesia explores further beyond these marvels of science.

The earliest human records make references to men and women who could find wells, springs, precious metals and many other things by divining or dowsing. It is one of the oldest known arts of China. In the dark and somber forests of the far north subarctic regions, the Finns have used pendulums or hazel twigs to discover the sex of an unborn child, to find water, etc. The simple, semiliterate early churchmen classified such arts too readily as the works of the devil whereas forcing those who would not accept Christianity to swallow a live snake apparently was not! Consequently few people dared practice openly a traditional father-to-son science or art, unless living hidden high in the mountains or deep in the forests.

At the close of the nineteenth century, an eminently respectable figure of the Catholic Church, Abbé Mermet, undertook careful scientific research upon the historical, practical and theoretical aspects of what came to be known in France as *radiesthésie*. This was the title of his famous book expounding the result of his research. In England the final *e* became an *a,* and the accent was dropped. The abbé, and some other colleagues of his cloth, conducted their experiments in such places as police stations. They found missing persons, diagnosed diseases and performed much that can only be described as almost miraculous.

Remarkable work was also done by the Reverend Jean Louis Bourdoux (1876–1963), a missionary father with the Third Order of St. Francis of Assisi (Albi) in the Matto Grosso jungles. He found it impossible to preach his faith without trying to heal the suffering and physical miseries of those natives who came to him for help. The only medicines available to him were the native herbs of the district, none of which he knew, as he had been born in France. Nor did he know anything about medical diagnosis or prognosis. All he had were his prayers and a knowledge of radiesthesia. He healed innumerable terrible tropical diseases, cases of syphilis, some lepers and many sick people whose ailments defied diagnosis. That he healed cancer was ignored by the medical profession. But most of us can accept the word of a Franciscan friar. His *Notions Pratiques de Radiesthésie pour les Missionaires* (Desforges, Paris) ran into many editions, and is still a great classic.

Now many people know that a diviner, dowser or radiesthesist employs either a hazel twig or a pendulum to detect something. What is not widely known is that the instrument used is exactly like the hands of a clock; it has no function at all except to show what the person has found. The sensitivity exists (or is absent) in the person who does the examination; it does not exist in whatever instrument is used to read the results from. There is just one drawback to this extraordinary science, on the evidence I have come across. Though many are born with the gift of being able to use radiesthesia, there are others who are not. The will to study may be there, but a quick course and good luck at exams do not help here, because one is not learning to use an instrument, one is learning to control and develop the self.

One faculty any would-be radiesthesist must have is the ability to detach himself entirely from the experiment in hand. Learning not to project one's thoughts into the pendulum is very much harder than it sounds. One must remember to conduct one's tests in neutral conditions. Take off a watch or metallic jewelry. Scissors, knives must be removed far from the test; ordinary alloy cutlery may cause an artificial gravitational force to affect the pendulum or instrument used in detection. Television, radio and stereo equipment also must be removed because they have active magnetic fields even when not playing. All of these are obviously logical disturbing factors. Equally disturbing, often more so, are tiredness, lack of vitality and doubts on the part of the operator (if inexperienced), skepticism on the part of other people present. All these factors render the learning of the science, even by a naturally gifted student, very challenging.

To overcome some of the difficulties which have to be mastered, it has been established that each individual must have a personally polarized pendulum which is the correct weight for him; the length of the thread from which it is suspended varies according to the vibrations of the individual operator, and may also vary according to the type of work undertaken. This important fact was discovered by Dr. Copen.

Most of the above remarks apply to a pendulum because this is generally easier to handle than the split hazel twig or other more advanced instruments such as the radameter. The instruments show the operator the radiations present in the subject matter being examined. The scope of this is seemingly unlimited.

For the beginner the pendulum swings in a circle. Dr. Copen has distinguished some forty different types of pendulum movements. Of these, there are movements which are basically positive, those which are neutral, and those which are negative. It was discovered at an early date that the pendulum showed distinctly different results for healthy and sick organisms and people.

Several volumes could be compiled to describe the enormous amount of painstaking research which radiesthesists of many countries have put into detailed observations of medical diagnosis and the health or sickness of the body, covering practically every ailment and minute condition of the body ever known to man.

Radiesthesia is an excellent method by which to determine which of the various healing arts is most suitable for different types of people, particularly in relation to their astrologically derived characteristics. Radiesthesia speeds up all forms of diagnosis, and since the exact number of vibrations (radiations) differs for each condition, an expert has less chance of making a mistake. This is encouraging because there are so many symptoms that are similar for different diseases.

The work of radiesthesia encompasses using very large numbers. These become exceedingly difficult for the operator to detect without moving the hand that holds the pendulum, because they take a long time to count. I give one of the easier examples from Pierre Beasse's classic textbook *Physical Radiesthesia:* 'Each series of oscillations is followed by a number of gyrations equal to the serial figure, and increases, each time, in an arithmetic progression, to a limit number, after which it starts again with the starting figure!' He quotes the following formula for gold: 11g.3.osc:11g.5.osc:11g.-7.osc:11g.9.osc:11g.11.osc.

If we contemplate the expertise and practice necessary to hold a human hand in a relaxed position, with no twitch of a muscle, while so many movements are made and counted, we soon come to see why the electronic version of radiesthesia, called radionics, just had to come into being. The original work was done by Albert Abrams, a medical man of the West Coast, who had a distinguished career as a neurologist. He was both curious in and attracted by radioactivity. He constructed on radiesthetic principles a notorious black box that could detect radiesthesia vibrations, and furthermore transmit corrected vibrations along a specific wavelength.

His expenses for such research work were extremely high. It is no wonder that he began to manufacture the black box, and issue one with instructional booklet to whomsoever could afford to purchase it. The American medical profession thought this was a profanation of the holy of holies; their righteous anger and sorrow exceeded that described by

Josephus when the Emperor Titus razed Jerusalem and destroyed the Temple. This was because whatever other attack had failed, medical authorities have always produced the old mystique of diagnosis: nobody, they crow, can diagnose but us, and here was this traitor from their own ranks breaking up one of the world's tightest monopolies!

Unfortunately for the critics, fortunately for history and science, Abrams' contraption worked. The British medical authorities, anxious to avoid the embarrassment that assailed their brethren across the Atlantic, sat in committee under the aegis of Lord Horder, one of the most widely respected men in the profession. His findings were that the box worked, although he, like many others, did not know how. He found that he could sense movements and changes occurring in his body when the box transmitted healing vibrations to him (he was suffering from an ulcer, I believe). I have, myself, sat in a room with a modern radionic computer, and felt the changes taking place in my body. The B.M.A. issued a noncommittal report. Privately, several doctors acquired machines for their own use.

It is one of the disadvantages of being an innovator that successors find the inventor's work comparatively clumsy in comparison with the improvements which they are able to make because of his work. Ruth Drown's version was more efficient, as was the De la Warr version. After the Second World War, Dr. Bruce Copen, with a flair for mathematics and a profound understanding of electronic engineering, produced the most efficient diagnostic and broadcasting instruments yet. Handy, transportable, transistorized and accurate beyond anything hitherto experienced, the new models attained a worldwide success. The Radionic Analytic Computer Mark II is the most advanced instrument available; it was designed to cover such involved things as auric rates, secretion rates, virus and bacteria tests, isotype sensitivity; an electronic vibro-potentizer has been built into the computer.

Training is needed to use them, for the instruments depend upon the operator. While they cut down the exhausting time which preradionic radiesthesia consumes, they still do not eliminate the operator, and if he does not have proper training he cannot substitute the machine for personal inefficiency.

But it is easier to teach people how to diagnose with a machine than by simple pendulum or rod, etc.

One of the drawbacks of all radiesthetic and radionic work resembles the curse of Cassandra. If a radiesthesist becomes in any way subjectively involved in the matter being examined, efficiency is lost; or put more simply, one cannot receive when one is transmitting. If you put out thoughts on your personal frequency, you cannot use that frequency to receive vibrations. This is the chief reason why most untrained people cannot use the instruments. It is incredible that medical men whose training takes five to six years on average so often believe that this qualifies them to master any technique, however far removed from their own, within days, if not minutes. I required several months' training before I considered myself capable of using a computer for diagnosis, but I knew one man who denounced the same machine as nonsense because he could not handle it within fifteen minutes: 'All you have to do is hold a pendulum over it,' he said. It may look that way, but there is much more to it than that.

In the hands of an expert, radionics is irreplaceable; without proper training it is almost useless. Professor Bruce and Dr. Lucy Copen have devoted most of their lives to research into radiesthesia and radionics.

49.

RAISIN CURE

One of the most exceptional men I have known was Dr. Josiah Oldfield, who when he was nearly a century old was as strong and full of life as a young man of twenty-five. He was once an allopathic doctor, saw the light and abandoned all artificial methods for God-made rather than man-made healing.

One of his favorite treatments was the simple but highly effective raisin cure. Take a packet of raisins (preferably without any chemicals added by the packers), put them in a basin, and fill this up with pure, filtered water, or natural water from a mountain stream or rainfall (provided that there is no suggestion of nuclear fall-out or pollution in the district). If possible, warm the water slightly before covering the raisins, then cover the basin with a clean piece of muslin or linen. Leave for two whole days. After this the raisins are eaten and the water is drunk. For one whole day the patient neither eats nor drinks anything but the raisins and their water.

The first mountain I climbed was the Säntis in eastern Switzerland. I was led up the gray rocks and over the snow by Kurt, and rather like Daudet's *Tartarin,* we despised those who had reached the peak by the *téléphérique.* While we enjoyed tomato sandwiches and white wine, Kurt told me that every spring his mother made the whole family spend two or three days eating nothing but grapes. Such a cure must have come down from the Roman times. (Raisins are simply dried grapes.)

50.

REICHIAN THERAPEUTICS

Wilhelm Reich (1897–1957) was born in Austria and trained as a doctor. A Freudian psychoanalyst, he developed his theories of orgone biophysics before the Second World War, and founded his Orgone Institute in New York in 1942. Discredited by the Federal Food and Drug Administration in 1954, he died tragically in prison. Reich's works on orgonomy have brought him international recognition, posthumously.

Throughout Europe and in some large American centers, the Reichian form of healing is gaining adherents. The basic theory is that all mental stresses, anxieties, neuroses and emotional conflicts are expressed unconsciously in the body. Loneliness, anger, secretiveness, suspicion and inability to trust or love others all manifest themselves, say the Reichian therapists, and they work upon the body to produce reactions in the physical medium which relate to the emotional state, conflict and inhibitions, etc. As the emotional release is effected, the relationship of mind and body is removed, and the cause for illness is removed.

The theory is extremely interesting. It is closely related to the psychosomatic school of psychology. Some practitioners apply their attention to the feet and reflex areas of the body. (See FOOT ZONE THERAPY.)

51.

RIKLI'S SUNSHINE CURE

It is strange today to think of Arnold Rikli (1823–1906) spending much of his life teaching people to let God's good sun shine upon their bodies. But it is stranger still if we research the period and find that at the time women might wear five or six petticoats, or more if they were rich!

From the time when Julian the Apostate ceased to be Emperor of Rome (A.D. 363), the human body ceased to be respectable, something created by divinity, and became as it were a snare set by the devil, a source of endless temptations. Popes, bishops, priests and rulers insisted that the body should be smelled rather than seen. Nineteenth-century missionaries did the same damage to the Polynesians whom they obliged to cover up all flesh with voluminous, drab textiles.

To stand up in public and teach people that health was to

be gained by taking off clothes and letting the sun touch their bodies was not only to risk cries of paganism, heresy and satanic practices, but to be in danger for one's own life and liberty.

In our time when beaches, riversides and meadows are garlanded with people of both sexes lying almost or wholly nude in the sun, it is fitting to remember one of the great pioneers of the health movement whose foresight, instinctive knowledge and courage made such a simple joy possible again.

52.

SAUNAS

An old Finnish proverb says that 'what sauna, spirits, and tar, will not cure is beyond help.' The true sauna (pronounced *sowna*) is a tradition going back to the earliest beginnings of Finnish culture. Most saunas nowadays are heated with an electric stove on which stones of a specific type are placed. These rocks have the property of retaining heat for long periods.

The true *Savu-sauna* is made by chopping up birch logs by hand, and very warming that is, and putting them into an enormous oven over which is piled a pyramid of the heat-retaining stones. The roof vent of the bathhouse is opened, the door is left open and the younger members of the family are placed on duty to see that the fire does not go out and that no sparks fly out to damage the surrounding forest. Plenty of logs are placed on it to heat up the stones.

After two or three hours the fire dies down, *'Kaikki hiilet pois,'* as they say. The vent is shut, the door is shut, and soon the family and guests come down, men first, women later, when the heat is not so fierce. Having disrobed, they enter into

the mouth of hell, for the heat always takes one's breath away
at first.

No sauna is beneficial unless it runs at 212° F. or more,
often reaching 248° F. I have sat in one that registered 284°
F., but not for very long! For a newcomer, 212° F. is quite
hot enough to begin with. The first in-sitting should last only
five minutes for beginners. Old hands will cheerfully stay
fifteen to twenty minutes before rushing out into the icy
waters of a lake, or failing that, as cold a shower as available.
Sauna without cold water defeats the purpose of the exercise,
and if you've been in a room correctly warmed, you'll welcome that cold water all right.

I remember being in northern Karelia in the middle of September, when the temperature fell to an average of 36° F.
every evening although the days were still comparatively
warm. We had a marvelous sauna by sunset. The entire lake
was aglow with the reds and purples of the sky, the water of
the lake stung our bodies like a million icy needles, but
we swam around impervious, our bodies were practically
steaming. I have rarely found myself so healthy in my life.

Generally one should not need to dry oneself all over after
a sauna, just a brief massage of the hair, and of any parts
which have been chilled or rheumatic before the sauna,
maybe, but the object is to tone up the skin and muscles so
that the blood circulation can open and shut the skin pores
more efficiently. The cleansing properties of a sauna amaze
all beginners, many of whom have never seen their skin so
pink and clean.

One illusion is that a sauna should be bone dry heat; this is
wrong. Finns always have a wooden bucket filled with water
in the room, a long-handled ladle, and from time to time they
sprinkle a ladle or two full of water onto the hot stones. The
resulting steam prevents the drying out of eyes, epithelial
cells, mucous membranes, lungs, etc. It is essential.

Associated with the sauna is the birch leaf *vihta,* a collection of twigs bound together in a traditional manner (not
with string) and used for a light massage of the body. In
some parts of Finland the bundle was of pine needles, or even
of juniper twigs, both of which sting more than birch twigs.
Viljo Issakainen, who was born in the province of Finland

seized by the Russians after the 1939 war, told me that in
eastern Karelia it was very common to use the pine, juniper
or rowan twigs, if birch were not available. They all add to
the therapeutic and stimulating value of the sauna.

For thousands of years Finnish women have gone into the
sauna to have their babies. Colds, headaches, aches, pains,
rheumatic pains, internal troubles, digestive disturbances and,
what is more, a whole range of psychosomatic upsets,
neuroses and anxieties disappear during their health-giving
heat.

It is unwise to start this treatment if there is any consti-
tutional weakness, heart trouble, diabetes in advanced state,
etc. In such conditions one might try a semisauna at 165° F.
to see how one feels before trying the full treatment. The
length of time spent in the heat should be measured by an experienced person.

In America and Western Europe there are many establishments which purport to be saunas but which are far from
it. Many are merely warm rooms in which people may sit and
read a magazine or make assignations. The heat of a real
sauna precludes both such activities.

CUPPING (*q.v.*) was usually applied in the sauna.

53.

SCHROTH THERAPY

Johann Schroth (1800–56) was a simple peasant farmer of
Schleswig Holstein who became one of the leading authorities
of the Reform school of therapy in Germany. He was an old
school friend of Priessnitz, the advocate of water therapy. He
achieved such exceptionally brilliant cures that the German
medical profession raised no objections when he was given
State authorization to practice! Since then, the reputation of

the Schroth clinics for healing serious diseases and morbid conditions has continued to benefit.

In contradistinction to his old comrade, Schroth developed the dry cure diet which gives preference to dry foods, and rigidly controls the amount of liquid intake allowed to the body so that there may take place a cleansing of the organs and blood, facilitating natural eliminative processes.

Damp packs are sometimes applied to the body during the treatment, but generally the internal organs are forced to produce their natural salivary-type fluids to dissolve the dry foods that are the main source of nourishment during the cure.

54.

SLEEP THERAPY

'Sleep,' said Byron, 'hath its own world, A boundary between the things misnamed death and existence.'

My father, T. J. H. Norman Law, a masseur and chiropodist, taught me, even in my boyhood, that a sick person must sleep because that gives time for spirit friends to bring healing and help to correct the vibrations. I owe a lot to his wisdom in such matters.

Schopenhauer put it this way: 'Sleep is to a man what winding is to a clock.' We all sleep, but how little most of us think about it. It has been shown that a more restful sleep comes to people in the Northern Hemisphere if they point their heads toward the North Magnetic Pole. In the Southern Hemisphere, sleep with the head to the South Pole.

Hans Georg Weidner did some serious research on the subject of mattresses. I quote: 'To most people the springs of the mattress base are, in any case, usually harmful, as they cause disturbances between the harmonious exchange processes which take place between the Cosmos and the Earth, and vice versa.' I have spent years camping in many countries, and I may say without fear or favor that when one has slept in our mother the Earth's bosom (to use the idiom of the American Indians) one awakens healthier and fresher than from any hotel super-spring mattress bed.

Field Marshal Jan Smuts always slept upon a hard wooden bed when he could not sleep on the soil of the Veldt. When he was a boy he rode off alone into the vast, untamed Veldt with horse, rifle, a blanket and a grammar of ancient Greek. When he returned seven days later he had memorized the entire grammar so perfectly that he could quote any of it upon request.

The coils of mattresses can transmit vibrations of a harmful nature (see RADIESTHESIA) because the coils are usually wound in negative directions. Furthermore they are often constructed of base-metal alloys that are dangerous to healthy, let alone sick, sleepers.

The human spine needs to relax during sleep. This it can do easily upon any hard surface which does not give at every movement, as all sprung mattresses do. A number of solutions is possible. One is to put a Lakhovsky-style copper (pure copper) coil round the bed, both expensive and difficult since it must be done by an expert radiesthesist. A second way is to discard the mattress, purchase a large piece of wood or chipboard ¾–1 inch thick and cover it with a layer of either foam rubber or esparto or marram grass. Heather would do if properly dried out. Bracken can be used but it has to be replaced more often. Many will imagine this to be an uncomfortable bed, but believe me, the depth of rest and relaxation gained from a hard surface is 100 per cent better than any spring bed.

It is a revolting custom to use a mattress somebody else has slept upon. It will be full of their emotional and hygienic radiations. It is not a bad idea when visiting hotels or other lodgings, to take a sheet of polythene and place it under the sheet upon which one lies.

If a person has been sick for a long time, it is wise to discard the mattress and replace it with one of the recommended substitutes. This must certainly be done with a mattress or bed upon which somebody has died. Feather mattresses and eiderdowns are best discarded also except where facilities exist for cleaning the feathers.

Kapok fiber is safe to use, and is becoming more popular; provided that no illness occurs, it could be used for ten years. Horsehair is to be avoided at all costs, especially as many horses are slaughtered in conditions of great fear and anguish. The vibrations emanating from the creatures during their last moments are reason enough not to use anything with such terrible, sorrowful radiations. It is important to note that some people feel that plastic foam rubber absorbs energy from them, so avoid it if you feel great tiredness. I always avoid nylon sheets; they upset my natural body currents terribly and make me feel very nervous. The coverings must never be so thick that they interfere with the natural respiration of the sleeper.

In my father's family there has been a strange superstition for many centuries that no Law should ever sleep with his feet pointing toward the door of the room or he will surely be carried out dead next morning. What historical event in our family that harks back to I do not know. I can only say this: I have an instinctive aversion to doing so, and cheerfully cause chaos in a hotel by changing all the furniture around to avoid it. Landladies at climbing resorts are used to me by now and give in to my whim about it.

The average human can go without food for a month and without liquids for between forty-eight and seventy-two hours. But to go without sleep is very dangerous for the nervous system. To miss sleep for four or five days is almost certain to cause damage which cannot be repaired.

Sleep is a great therapeutical agent. A person who cannot sleep will never get well. Generally it is best to sleep on the right side, left hand folded on the right hand in front of the head, slightly below it. One may cover the head lightly—but never the nose and mouth—with a sheet. The body naturally changes the position without awakening us during a night's sleep.

Never take a problem to bed. You'll solve nothing before the morning, and if you did, what could you do about it while everybody else is in the land of Nod?

If you have a strenuous physical job, try to get fifteen minutes' nap during the lunch break, which will do you more good than alcoholic drinks.

If you cannot sleep well, take a glass of warm (not boiled) milk, add a teaspoonful of pure honey and a pinch of cinnamon. I have never known that to fail. One pupil told me he read Professor X's books. When I asked why, he replied, 'They're so boring I fall asleep after one or two sentences.'

Cats have a tranquil disposition. They also have the capacity to sleep a short while any time of the day, as could Winston Churchill.

'Sleep before 12 gives you more benefit than any sleep after it,' my mother used to insist. In effect, what is meant is that you should sleep as soon as you feel tired. To go on long after you feel tired is bad for your nervous system. It is not possible to sleep with dusk and awake at sunrise, especially in a block of flats or without central heating.

Although it is good and healthy to sleep with an open window, this does not necessitate allowing a Force 10 gale to blow through the room. It does not require you to allow fog and damp to enter the room either. It does not preclude warming the bed with hot-water bottles or electric blankets (I prefer the former to the latter). Never sleep with heating aids in the bed once the bed is warm. If you heat the bedroom with central heating or any other system, do ensure that proper ventilation comes into the room so that stuffiness, dryness and burning-up of oxygen do not take place. Do not fall for all this Spartan toughness nonsense, which is overdone.

I often eat an apple or an orange just before sleep, and may enjoy one or two chapters of travel books or poetry before closing my eyes with a final prayer of thanksgiving.

The first famous sleeper was Epimenides, a Greek poet, who is said to have fallen asleep as a boy in a mystic cave, awaking only fifty-seven years later fully enlightened. The legend of the Sleeping Beauty comes originally from Charles Perrault's *Contes* published in the mid-seventeenth century.

55

SPIRITUAL HEALING

This term is applied to a number of different forms which on the surface seem very different.

Divine Healing. Many healers who operate within the established Christian churches believe that their gift comes directly from God or from the Christ. They attune themselves through prayer and consider themselves to be channels for the divine healing power. Most healing of this kind is done by relatively untrained groups of people or by a handful of charismatic evangelical healers like Kathryn Kuhlman or Oral Roberts. An interest in healing is, however, returning to the established churches, and in many countries there are groups working to encourage the development of what they regard to be a latent gift that most people possess. Some of the well-known healers in Britain consider themselves to be faith healers rather than psychic healers, but the results of their work seem to belie any distinction made.

Psychic Healing. In principle the difference of this to divine healing is the label. Clearly, many religious people would prefer to believe that healing comes direct from God than through the intermediary of a highly developed discarnate soul. Many healers, however, are spiritualists and believe that they are being "used" by a higher entity who once lived in a body.

The National Federation of Spiritual Healers in England and the Spiritual Frontiers Fellowship in America have well-regarded training courses for people who wish to develop their potential for healing.

One of the most remarkable psychic healers was Edgar Cayce (1887–1944), whose work is probably better documented than that of any other healer. A Kentucky Sunday school teacher, he practiced complex and accurate medi-

cal diagnosis in trance for forty-three years, usually without
having met the patient. He left stenographic reports of thirty
thousand of these diagnoses, along with hundreds of complete
case reports, containing affidavits by the patients and reports
by physicians. He was not, however, a spiritualist.

Psychic Surgery. A lot of interest has been created in recent
years by reports of the psychic surgeons of Brazil and the
Philippines. José Arigo of Brazil operated illegally for years,
but was so successful that he had a hospital built for him.

Tony Agapoa has achieved remarkable documented cures
of medically incurable patients suffering from cancer. He can
apparently open the body without surgical instruments to cut,
or anesthetic or pain for the patient. Dr. Sigrun Seutemann
lived three years in the Philippines, and witnessed some seven
thousand operations by psychosurgery faith healers. Some
were also witnessed by Dr. Lyall Watson. There are about
thirty-eight such healers there.

George Chapman in Aylesbury, a retired fireman, is said to
perform skillful psychic surgery while under the spirit control
of a London surgeon named Dr. William Lang, who died in
1937.

There is no doubt that spiritual healing has restored life to
thousands of desperately ill people who were given up by
allopathic medicine. In Britain, accredited spiritual healers
are allowed to treat patients in state hospitals. It is interesting
that most spiritual healers refuse payment for their treatment.

56.

SWIMMING AS THERAPY

Swimming has many more uses than enjoyment. Apart from
being a method of saving one's own life, it has a profound
effect upon the entire physical structure of the swimmer—his

muscles, internal organs, nervous system and mental processes.

The man who did most to develop the theory of swimming as a therapeutic art was the coach Reg Brickett, who had patients sent along to him by Harley Street specialists who recognized the curative properties of swimming. This brilliant man taught me to observe how the water supported weakened, injured muscles better than the thinner medium of air could hold them in position on land.

Several people I know who have had a lot of rheumatic pains and the like have declared themselves much healthier when they went swimming twice a week. Generally they swim in warmed water indoor pools, but I do know of a couple of people who hardened themselves, starting in the summer, to swim a few minutes a day in the sea all the year round.

The mineral content of sea water is the same as that of the human blood, so unpolluted sea water is itself most therapeutic. However, many councils of watering places are quite content to let the town sewage gurgle out to sea, a mile or so offshore, where every tide can sweep it back to the beach and the hapless bathers.

If swimming in a lonely place away from frequented beaches, there are a few precautions which have to be observed:

1) Swim diagonally across a bay, never try to fight a strong tide or current.
2) Swim parallel to the shore, never out to sea.
3) There are such forces as undertow and currents that can pull an inexperienced swimmer farther out than he or she anticipated. (Further useful hints are given in my *Beginner's Guide to Swimming and Water Sports*.)
4) Do avoid swimming alone unless you are extremely proficient.

The sea is at all times deceptive. I once found myself being carried rapidly out into the Black Sea when swimming off the Turkish coast. Then there are times when I have swum in the Arctic Ocean; even on a hot summer day the water is warm enough inshore, but even a short distance offshore there has frequently been an icy chill that all but numbs the brain as well as the mere muscles.

A brisk, short toweling with a fairly rough towel should be all that is needed to dry oneself after a swim. If feasible, a short run and some exercises on the sandy shore are better to tone up the body than a toweling, although the head may still be toweled to get the hair dry.

57.

TEMPERATURE DIAGNOSIS

Most modern homes have a thermometer, and it is by no means difficult to use one.

The human nervous system contains a thermostat which operates so that the output of heat by the muscles and from the combustion of food is perfectly balanced by loss of heat from the skin area. The average healthy human body heat extends from 98.4° Fahrenheit up to 99°, when measured in the mouth. Readings under the armpit are frequently as much as 1° lower than those of the mouth, and allowance should be made. The thermometer must be cleaned before use by immersion in some substance such as 10 per cent tincture of myrrh and water, or in pure witch hazel. After reading it must again be cleaned in the same way before being put away.

A high temperature is indicative of fever. This is the body's own healthy mechanism fighting off alien organisms which are trying to grow in a condition which is favorable to them. It is seldom desirable to try to reduce the temperature speedily. Herbal drinks that can encourage the body to expel the dead organisms, which also takes physical effort after the body has defeated them, are very helpful.

A patient with an emotional disturbance, fretting, anger,

etc., will often cause a temperature to soar two or three degrees higher than normal (especially a willful child). This can be compensated for by checking the temperature frequently.

A consistently high temperature is a sign that something is out of order with the patient, and a record of the date and time (morning, midday and evening) of readings should be kept. Expect slightly lower temperatures in the morning, and slightly higher temperatures in the evening. If temperature rises and stays for more than a day above 105° you should seek expert advice; 107° calls for immediate action because the situation is getting very serious. But many people have had temperatures of 110° for a few days and still rallied around. A very rapid rise in temperature in an old person who has been sick for some time may indicate the approach of the end of their incarnation.

Here are some diseases with their characteristic temperatures. Diphtheria shows a temperature around 103°; enteric fever shows an average 103°–105° during its height. In malaria the temperature rises during the hot stage to about 105°. In measles the range is from 99° in its early stages to 105° at the peak, and in pneumonia it is from 99° to 103°. In rheumatic fever the temperature roams from 101° to 103°. In tubercular cases the temperature generally ranges from 98.4° to 102°.

If the temperature falls below the average, this may be due, for example, to loss of blood, Bright's disease, diabetes, exposure (alpine), myxedema, peritonitis. The patient should be helped back to warmth, but air must never be excluded. Remember that too many blankets cut off oxygen from the body.

58.

TONGUE DIAGNOSIS

Although most allopaths ask patients to show them their tongue when ill, less use is made of the knowledge than it is by biochemists of the Schüssler system.

In the *New Era Biochemical Handbook* a detailed list is given showing most carefully which of the essential body salts is deficient if the tongue is such and such a color, if the density of the furring is too thick. If the tongue is furred obviously something is wrong with the entire mucous membrane (see MUCOUS-FREE DIET). APPLE CIDER VINEGAR (*q.v.*) can be used in some cases. Careful attention to diet is essential (see DIETETICS).

59.

URINE ANALYSIS

It is possible to purchase strips of porous papers that contain different chemical constituents. These make it possible to analyze urine by four different tests in about thirty seconds flat. The urine's chemical contents react differently to the four test materials. One of the chemicals in the papers measures the degree of alkalinity or acidity present; the others indicate whether there is an excess of protein, blood, etc., in the sample.

Persistent (not occasional) glucose in the urine indicates diabetes. If there is consistent showing of protein in urine then the kidneys are malfunctioning. The presence of bile in the urine indicates that the liver is not working well. If there is blood, great care must be taken to find out the source of the bleeding, and further tests must be done. The presence of pus in the urine shows that there is an infection of the urinary tract, and this may be serious. It is possible to make a further test with a hydrometer to obtain the exact specific gravity of the urine, which helps us understand the condition of the kidneys better.

Within a twenty-four-hour period a healthy man passes normally about fifty ounces of urine. The quantity is considerably increased if there has been heavy drinking, so there is no need to jump at pathological conditions. The cause of increase may be diabetes mellitus insipidus, chronic interstitial nephritis, high blood pressure, dropsical effusions or some nervous disorders such as hysteria. A decrease in the quantity is common in cases of fevers, low blood pressure, diarrhea, cholera, acute or chronic parenchymatous nephritis.

The color of urine in a state of health is a pale yellow. When there is diabetes it becomes extremely pale, even colorless. If it is brownish or reddish there is blood in the urine; if little blood is present the urine may show a smoke-like color. If it is orange it may not be due to fever or jaundice, but solely to excessively hard work. Very yellow urine indicates a presence of bile and probable liver disorders. Opalescent urine contains micro-organisms, or matter in a state of liquid suspension. Whitish, milky urine indicates chyle, fats or pus. Bluish urine may be due to typhus or poisoning from methylene blue. Greenish urine comes from heavy bile, creosote or coal tar in the system. Blackish urine indicates overdoses of coal tar derivatives, guaiacol creosote and liver disorders.

The odor of urine is also informative. Normally remarkable and slightly sharp to the nose, it intensifies if there is any acetone being micturated with it. It becomes unpleasantly ammoniacal if it is decomposing. It may smell like fresh violets if the patient has been absorbing turpentine.

Persistent scalding symptoms during micturating should be attended to at once, since this is sometimes a sign of gonorrhea. Do consult an expert.

60.

YOGA

The material in this section was researched and prepared by Albert Christian, D.G.A., F.I.A.L., M.Ph.A. I wish to acknowledge my gratitude to him for his help.

The earliest discovered textbook on yoga was compiled rather than written by Pantanjali about 250 B.C., but there are distinct references to it in the Sanskrit of Yajnavalkya, c. 1200 B.C. While the age of a system neither guarantees its respectability nor its accuracy, its durability over so many centuries makes it worthy of study.

Pantanjali described the meaning of the Sanskrit word *yoga* as harmony between the self and the source of spiritual power. This is the avowed objective of the system. It consists of the three stages, Meditation, Contemplation and Absorption, and there are six forms in which it is found.

Here are some of the *yogas*.

Bhakti yoga, the seeking of a pathway through devotion and love: in India this is linked with the cult of Vishnu.

Mantra yoga, primarily linked with the worship of Krishna, and principally concerned with the vibrations and radiations in life, much associated with musically minded seekers.

Karma yoga, the seeking of the pathway through the service of others. This is service in action, and it emphasizes the need to live in the present world and make the best of it. No tilting at windmills or quixotic slaying of winebag giants!

Jnana yoga, the path sought through the aspiration of the intellect.

Layakriya yoga, the seeking of a pathway through the contemplation and exploration of sexual relationships; the Hindu
equivalent of Freud, with a touch of Fraser (*The Golden
Bough*) and Jung (*Wandlungen und Symbole der Libido*) as
well.

Raja yoga, a complicated mixture of some of the above.

Hatha yoga, which is principally concerned with the health
of, and the mind's successful mastery of, the body. The doctrine of Chakras, centers of being, akin to acupuncture lines
of life force, comes under Hatha yoga.

One of the drawbacks of the system is that it is taught in
various forms by wandering gurus (the word means a
dispeller of darkness), whose quality is so varied that they
raise confusion (if not doubt) in the minds of those who are
not ardent disciples.

Some forms of yoga and some gurus have enjoyed unprece-
dented success as a vogue among bored city dwellers in the
last three decades. Inasmuch as many would not accept any
simple morals or home truths from their own local priests
(of any denomination), the effect of yoga teaching has often
been beneficent.

The beginner is encouraged to spend considerable time in
the practice of breathing exercises (see BREATHING and
AIR THERAPY). The divergencies in the system do not usually exclude the need for some strenuous and uncomfortable
exercises in a sitting position. They are well-suited for a very
hot climate in which violent physical exercise or gymnastics
might induce illness rather than health, and for sedate, middle-aged people who have never indulged in much exercise or
games during their youth.

The role and goal of yoga seem equally obscure. The study
is fraught with philosophical terms that are difficult to define,
and which do not translate very well from Sanskrit or Prakrit,
much less Hindu or Bengali. The search for contentment
often seems hard to distinguish from cow-like placidity and
nonchalance, but this confusion is rather the fault of the guru
or disciple (*chela*) than of the doctrine. Seated naked in the
Himalayas it is easy, perhaps, to rid oneself of all desires, but
in a Westernized civilization, surrounded by advertisements,

the exercise may be too much for normal flesh and blood to bear.

Most true yogis insist upon cleanliness, self-discipline and a willed control of the thoughts in the pupil before they consent to teach him. In its higher aspects yoga is near to phrenosophy, which advises its followers not to sit down and wish for a better house, but to direct their thoughts to what they should do to get a better house.

Many yogis insist upon disciples becoming vegetarians. This often means a deficiency in protein foods, since few vegetables contain enough of the known twenty-two amino-acids to constitute a good meal. Again this regime is safer to follow in a hot climate than in a cold, wet, temporal zone of the earth.

Owing to the decentralized nature of yoga, the system tends to get tangled up with woolly, unproductive thinking. We should remember that time is life, for when there is no more time left to us, we leave our bodies whether we have learned anything or not. Spiritual acrobatics and circus tricks do not make a doctrine more true. It is impressive to see a man dug up after being buried alive for forty days, alive after swallowing sulphuric acid, but the connection between the miracle and the doctrine is not so easily proven.

Anybody who decides to follow this as a therapy may well receive a lot of help from it and from some of the gurus who would be a credit to any doctrine they preached. However, there are a lot of less worthy teachers, and the system is by no means a panacea.

Part three

GOING FURTHER

SUGGESTIONS
FOR FURTHER READING

Health Research Publishers
Box 70
Mokelumne Hill, Calif. 95245

This publishing house reproduces antiquated and public domain works. Though many of the books are filled with obvious errors in spelling, printing and information, they make accessible a wealth of obscure and hard-to-find information. All their books are spiral bound, and range in price from $4.00 to $20.00.

PART I

Carrel, Alexis. *Man the Unknown*. New York: Harper & Row, 1939.

Carson, Rachel. *The Sea Around Us*. New York: Oxford University Press, 1961.

Jarvis, D. C. *Folk Medicine*. New York: Fawcett World Library, 1973.

Pappworth, Maurice. *Human Guinea Pigs*. Boston: Beacon Press, 1968.

Turner, J. S. *The Chemical Feast*. New York: Grossman, 1970.

PART II

1. ACUPUNCTURE AND MOXIBUSTION

Austin, Mary. *Acupuncture Therapy*. ASI Pubs., Inc., 1972.

Hashimoto, M. *Japanese Acupuncture*. New York: Liveright, 1968.

Lawson-Wood, D. *Five Elements of Acupuncture and Chinese Massage*. New York: British Book Center, Inc., 1973.

Mann, Felix. *Acupuncture, the Ancient Chinese Art of Healing*. Peter Smith.

——. *Acupuncture*, rev. ed. New York: Random House, 1973.

Moss, Louis. *Acupuncture and You*. Secaucus, N.J.: Citadel Press, 1972.

2. THE ALEXANDER METHOD

Barlow, Wilfred. *The Alexander Technique*. New York: Knopf, 1973.

Maisel, E. *The Alexander Technique*. New York: University Books, Inc., 1969.

4. APPLE CIDER VINEGAR AND HONEY

Jarvis, D. C. *Folk Medicine*. New York: Fawcett World, 1973.

——. *Arthritis and Folk Medicine*. New York: Fawcett World, 1974.

5. AURAS

Kilner, W. J. *Aura*. New York: Weiser, 1965.

8. BIOCHEMISTRY

Chapman, J. B. *Dr. Schussler's Biochemistry*. Formur International, 1975.

Powell, Eric F. *Biochemistry Up to Date*. Formur International, 1975.

13. COLOR THERAPY

* Heline. *Colour Therapy, Healing and Regeneration Through Color*. Oceanside, Calif.: New Age Press.

15. COUÉ'S AUTOSUGGESTION

Baudouin, C. *Suggestion and Autosuggestion*. Norwood Editions, 1920.

Coué, Émile. *Self-Mastery Thru Autosuggestion*. Wehman, 1968.

17. DIETETICS AND VITAMINS

Clements, F. W., and Rogers, Josephine F. *Food and Diet for Family Health.* Reed, 1972.

Davidson, Stanley. *Human Nutrition and Dietetics,* 6th rev. ed. New York: Longman, 1975.

Fiore, Evelyn, ed. *Low Carbohydrate Diet.* New York: Grosset & Dunlap, 1965.

Krause, Marie V., and Hunscher, Martha A. *Food, Nutrition and Diet Therapy.* Philadelphia, Pa.: W. B. Saunders Co., 1972.

Williams, Sue R. *Nutrition and Diet Therapy.* St. Louis, Mo.: C. V. Mosby Co., 1973.

18. EYE DIAGNOSIS (IRIDOLOGY)

* Jensen. *The Science and Practice of Iridology.* Escondido, Calif.: Jensen Publications.

21. FINGERNAIL DIAGNOSIS

Benham. *Laws of Scientific Hand Reading.* New York: Duell, Sloan & Pearce, 1966.

Jaquin. *The Hand of Man.* India: Sager Pub., 1967.

Law, Donald. *Astrology, Palmistry and Dreams.* Totowa, N.J.: Littlefield, Adams & Co., 1975.

22. FOODS THAT DECEIVE US

* Abrahamson & Pezet. *Body, Mind and Sugar.* New York: Pyramid, 1971.

* Hurd. *Ten Talents Cook Book.* Grand Rapids, Mich.: Life Line Health Center.

* Shelton. *Food Combining Made Easy.* San Antonio, Tex.: Sheltons, 1973.

* ———. *Superior Nutrition.* San Antonio, Tex.: Sheltons, 1972.

27. HERBALISM

* Clymer. *Nature's Healing Agents.* Philadelphia, Pa.: Dorrance, 1963.

* Krochmal, Arnold. *Guide to Medicinal Plants of the U.S.* New York: Quadrangle, 1973.

Law, Donald. *Concise Herbal Encyclopedia.* New York: St. Martin's, 1974.

———. *Herb Growing for Health.* New York: Arco, 1969.

———. *Herbs for Cooking and Healing.* N. Hollywood, Calif.: Wilshire.

* Millspaugh. *American Medicinal Plants.* New York: Dover, 1974.

Simmonite, W. J., and Culpeper, N. *Herbal Remedies.* Hackensack, N.J.: Wehman, 1957.

* Vogel. *American Indian Medicine.* Norman: University of Oklahoma Press, 1970.

28. HOMEOPATHY

Puddephatt, Noel. *First Steps of Homeopathy.* St. Louis, Mo.: Formur International, 1975.

29. HYPNOSIS FOR HEALING AND DIAGNOSIS

Ambrose, Gordon, and Newbold, George. *Handbook of Medical Hypnosis.* Baltimore, Md.: Williams & Wilkins, 1968.

Baudouin, Charles. *Suggestion and Autosuggestion.* Norwood, Pa.: Norwood Editions, 1920.

Check, David B., and Lecron, Leslie M. *Clinical Hypnotherapy.* New York: Grune & Stratton, 1968.

Kroger, William S. *Clinical and Experimental Hypnosis.* New York: Lippincott, 1963.

34. MIRACLE CURES

Eddy, Mary Baker. *Science and Health, with Key to Scripture.* Boston: First Church of Christ, Scientist.

Kuhlman, Kathryn. *I Believe in Miracles.* Englewood Cliffs, N.J.: Prentice-Hall, 1962.

Long, M. *The Secret Science Behind Miracles.* Los Angeles: DeVorss, 1948.

Richardson, Alan. *Miracle Stories of the Gospels.* Naperville, Ill.: Alec R. Allevson, 1941.

Werfel, Franz. *The Song of Bernadette.* New York: Avon Books, 1975.

37. NATURE CURE

Benjamin, Harry. *Everybody's Guide to Nature Cure*. New York: British Book Center, 1976.

39. OCCUPATIONAL THERAPY

Jones, M. *Approach to Occupational Therapy*. Reading, Pa.: Butterworths Pub., Inc.

Mountford, Stella. *Introduction to Occupational Therapy*. New York: Longman, Inc., 1971.

Willard, Helen, and Spackman, C. *Occupational Therapy*. New York: Lippincott, 1970.

43. PHYSICAL CULTURE AS THERAPY

Johnson, D. G., and Heidenstamm, O. *Modern Body Building*. Buchanan, N.Y.: Emerson Books, Inc.

44. PHYSIOTHERAPY

Cash, J. E. *Chest, Heart and Vascular Disorders for Physiotherapy*. New York: Lippincott, 1975.

Reilly and Brod. *The Edgar Cayce Handbook for Health Through Drugless Therapy*. New York: Macmillan, 1975.

46. PSYCHOMETRY

Butler, W. E. *How to Develop Psychometry*. New York: Samuel Weiser, Inc.

Nunnally, J. C. *Psychometry Theory*. New York: McGraw-Hill, 1967.

47. PSYCHOSOMATIC HEALING

Kissen, D. M. (ed.). *Psychosomatic Aspects of Neoplastic Diseases*. New York: Lippincott, 1964.

Ludwig, A. O., et al. *Psychosomatic Aspects of Gynecological Disorders*. Cambridge, Mass.: Harvard University Press, 1969.

Pierloot, R. *Recent Researches in Psychosomatics*. White Plains, N.Y.: Albert J. Phiebig, 1970.

Sargant, W. *Battle for the Mind*. New York: Harper & Row, 1971.

* Simeons, A. T. W. *Man's Presumptuous Brain*. New York: Dutton, 1961.

48. RADIESTHESIA AND RADIONICS

Tansley, David. *Radionics and the Subtle Anatomy of Man*. Weiser.

Tomlinson. *Medical Divination*. Surrey, England: Health Science, 1966.

Westlake. *Pattern of Health*. Berkeley, Calif.: Shambhala Pub., Inc., 1973.

Wethered. *The Practice of Medical Radiesthesia*. London: Fowler, 1967.

50. REICHIAN THERAPEUTICS

Reich, Wilhelm. *Character Analysis*. New York: Farrar, Straus & Giroux.

———. *Cancer Biopathy*. New York: Farrar, Straus & Giroux.

———. *Invasion of Compulsory Sex-Morality*. New York: Farrar, Straus & Giroux.

———. *Listen, Little Man!* New York: Farrar, Straus & Giroux.

———. *Mass Psychology of Fascism*. New York: Farrar, Straus & Giroux.

———. *Murder of Christ*. New York: Farrar, Straus & Giroux.

———. *Reich Speaks of Freud*. New York: Farrar, Straus & Giroux.

———. *Sexual Revolution*. New York: Farrar, Straus & Giroux.

———. *Function of the Orgasm*. Beaverton, Ore.: Touchstone Press, 1974.

———. *Selected Writings of Wilhelm Reich*. New York: Noonday Press, 1973.

52. SAUNAS

Viherjuuri, H. J. *The Sauna: The Finnish Bath*. Brattleboro, Vt.: Stephen Greene Press, 1965.

55. SPIRITUAL HEALING

Hammond, Sally. *We Are All Healers.* New York: Harper & Row, 1973.

Sugrue, Thomas. *There Is a River: The Story of Edgar Cayce.* New York: Dell, 1970.

Turner, Gordon. *Outline of Spiritual Healing.* New York: Warner Books, Inc., 1972.

Valentine, Tom. *Psychic Surgery.* New York: Pocket Books, 1975.

60. YOGA

Bernard, Theos. *Hatha Yoga.* Weiser, 1970.

Bhishu, Y. *Bhakti Yoga.* Des Plaines, Ill.: Toga Publication Society.

Frederic, L. *Yoga Assanas.* Hackensack, N.J.: Welman Bros.

Hittleman, Richard. *Yoga for Physical Fitness.* New York: Warner Books, 1974.

Iyengar, B. K. S. *Light on Yoga.* New York: Schocken Books Inc., 1972.

Krishna, Gopi. *Biological Basis of Religion and Genius.* New York: Harper & Row, 1972.

———. *Kundalini.* Westminster, Md.: Shambhala Pubns., 1973.

———. *The Secret of Yoga.* New York: Harper & Row.

Wood, E. *Yoga.* Baltimore, Md.: Penguin Books.

* Especially recommended.

WHERE TO GO
FOR RELIABLE INFORMATION

This is an information list, and the publisher in no way advocates, endorses or promotes any individual or group listed herein. List compiled exclusive of original author through United Communication Research Publications, GPO Brooklyn, New York 11202.

SPIRITUALIST CAMPS AND/
OR ASSOCIATIONS

These groups have contact with individuals engaged in either teaching or doing the following techniques: Auras, Color Therapy, Coué's Autosuggestion, Jewels as Therapeutic Agent, Miracle Cures, Music as Therapy, Phrenology, Psychometry, Sleep Therapy and Spiritual Healing.

However, one must be aware that in England, unlike in the United States, there is a free system with regard to the alternative practice of medicine, whereby an individual may practice most every technique discussed in this book without having to be concerned about government harassment. Of course, this does have its drawbacks, as there are many who practice who literally are unqualified and should not be allowed to tend to the sick. Be that as it may, here in the United States the pendulum has swung to the other extreme, and it is quite against the law for an unlicensed practitioner to practice medicine, regardless of how qualified he may be. Therefore you must keep in mind that:

No unlicensed individual is going to risk arrest, and you must not ask him either to prescribe for or treat an ailment.

You must thoroughly check all the camps and/or groups before you decide on any one individual, as most groups are quite cliquish.

You must trust your own feelings regarding any group or individual, licensed or unlicensed, and do not be dissuaded by talk or theatrical array. Be leery of any individual who claims a cure for anything.

Spiritual Frontiers Fellowship, 800 Custer Ave., Evanston, Ill. 60202

Foundation of Truth, 270-15th St. N.E., Atlanta, Ga. 30309

Silver Belle Association, Ephrata, Pa. 17522

Lily Dale Association, Lily Dale, N.Y. 14752

Order of St. Luke's, 19 S. 10th Street, Philadelphia, Pa. 19107

Inner Vision, Inc., 235 E. 22nd Street, New York, N.Y. 10010

Universal Spiritualist Association, Box 158, Chesterfield, Ind. 46017

New Jersey Parapsychology Forum, 296 Brook Lake Rd., Florham Park, N.J. 07932

Christian Spiritual Alliance, Inc., Lakemont, Ga. 30552. (Publication: *Orion Magazine*.)

Inner Light Foundation, Box 761, Novato, Calif. 94947. (Betty Bethards.)

National Spiritualist Association, Box 128, Cassadaga, Fla. 32706

CLASSES ON NATURAL HEALING

San Andreas Health Council, 531 Cowper St., Palo Alto, Calif. 94301

Wholistic Health and Nutrition Institute, 150 Shoreline Hwy., Mill Valley, Calif. 94941

Ananda Meditation Retreat, Allegheny Star Rt., Nevada City, Calif. 95959

New Morning Foundation, 2100 E. Speedway, Tucson, Ariz. 95716

Boston Center for the Healing Arts, 1 Park Pl., Boston, Mass. 02130

Boulder Center for the Healing Arts, 855 Arapahoe, Boulder, Colo.   80302

Center for Healing Studies, Old Sash Mill, 303 Portrero, Bldg. 19, Santa Cruz, Calif.   95060

MAIL ORDER

The following publishers and stores have a large selection of books on these subjects. Write for catalogues.

Health Research Publishers, Box 70, Mokelumne Hill, Calif.   95245

Aurora Books, Box 5852, Denver, Colo.   80217

Tao Books, 303-B Newberry St., Boston, Mass.   02115

Samuel Weisers, 734 Broadway, New York, N.Y.   10003

Yes Inc., 1030 31st Street N.W., Washington, D.C.   20007

1. Acupuncture and Moxibustion

Acupuncture Society of America, 3938 Main St., Kansas City, Mo.   64111

National Acupuncture Research Society, 505 Park Ave., New York, N.Y.   10036 (800) 223-5681

Traditional Acupuncture Foundation, c/o Center for Traditional Acupuncture, Inc., American City Bldg., Columbia, Md.   21044

2. The Alexander Method (Groups in this listing are accredited by main organization.)

American Center for the Alexander Technique, Inc., 142 W. End Ave., New York, N.Y.   10023 (212) 799-0468

California Center for the Alexander Technique, 931 Elizabeth St., San Francisco, Calif.   94114 (415) 282-8967; 811 23rd St., Santa Monica, Calif.   90403 (213) 451-3641 (Contact centers for training and teachers.)

3. Air Therapy (See Nature Cure.)

4. Apple Cider Vinegar and Honey

As suggested by the author, you may wish to contact the ARE (below) for further information on Edgar Cayce's use of this combination.

Association for Research and Enlightenment, Box 595, Atlanta Ave., Virginia Beach, Va. 23451. (Also publishes a newsletter based on Edgar Cayce's teachings.)

5. *Auras*

Rev. Noel Street, c/o Lotus Ashram, 128 N.E. 82nd Terrace, Miami, Fla. 33138. (Aura reader and healer.)

Rev. Beth Hand, 100 Union St., Mantua, N.J. 08051. (Healing and Auric readings.)

(See Spiritualist Camps listing for further information.)

Dr. Thelma Moss Center for Health Sciences, University of California, Los Angeles, Calif. 90024.

Scientific Research with Kirlian Photography photographing the auras of living and non-living things. (See Galaxies of Life published by Gordon & Breach Science Publishers, Inc., 1 Park Avenue, New York, N.Y. 10016.)

Inner Vision, Inc. (See Spiritualist Camps listing.)

Foundation Church (See Spiritualist Camps listing.)

6. *Bach's Flower Remedies* Preparations may be obtained through A. Nelson and Co. Ltd., 73 Duke St., Grosvenor Sq., London WIM 6BY, England.

Although they may not be very responsive, you may try to obtain information direct from The Dr. Bach Healing Center, Mount Vernon, Sotwell, Wallingford, Berks., England.

8. *Biochemistry* (Most health food stores stock Biochemic tissue salts.)

9. *Bircher-Müesli* (Ingredients obtainable through most health food stores.)

10. *Breathing Therapy*

Most yoga centers (see Yoga) teach some form of breath control; however, specific information and/or instruction is available through:

Ajapa Breath Foundation, 4801 Draper Ave., Montreal, Canada (514) 486-2844

Integral Yoga Institute, 500 W. End Ave., New York, N.Y. 10000 (212) 874-7500

3HO c/o Guru Ram Dass Ashram, 1620 Preuss Rd., Los Angeles, Calif. 90035 (213) 273-9422

11. Chiropody (Podiatry)

American Podiatric Association, 20 Chevy Chase Circle N.W., Washington, D.C. 20015. (National contact center for local practitioners and association [202] 362-2700.) National schools are:

California College of Podiatric Medicine, 1770 Eddy, San Francisco, Calif. 94115

Illinois College of Podiatric Medicine, 1001 N. Dearborn St., Chicago, Ill. 60610

New York College of Podiatric Medicine, 53 E. 124th St., New York, N.Y. 10035

Ohio College of Podiatric Medicine, 2057 Cornell Rd., Cleveland, Ohio 54106

SUNY School of Podiatric Medicine, Stonybrook, N.Y. 11790

Pennsylvania College of Podiatric Medicine, Race and 8th Sts., Philadelphia, Pa. 19107

12. Chiropractic: (Local practitioners and/or associations may be found in most yellow pages under title.)
Major national schools are:

Cleveland College of Chiropractic, 3511 W. Olympic Blvd., Los Angeles, Calif. 90019

Columbia College of Chiropractic, Box 167, Glen Head, N.Y. 11451

Logan College of Chiropractic, 130 Schoettler Rd., Chesterfield, St. Louis County, Mo. 63017

National College of Chiropractic, 200 E. Roosevelt Rd., Lombard, Ill. 60148

Palmer College of Chiropractic, 1000 Brady St., Davenport, Iowa 52803

Sherman College of Chiropractic, Box 5502, Springfield Rd., Spartanburg, S.C. 29301

Parker Chiropractic Research Foundation, Box 40444, Fort Worth, Tex. 76140

Western States College of Chiropractic, 2900 N.E. 132nd Ave., Portland, Ore. 97230

13. *Color Therapy* (Also see Spiritualist Camps listing.)
Mary Bassano, 275 Lake Oak Pl., Bricktown, N.J. 08723. (Teacher and color therapist as well as information source.)
Inner Light Foundation (See Spiritualist Camps listing.)
Christos School of Natural Healing (See Nature Cure [Clinics].)
Inner Vision, Inc. (See Spiritualist Camps listing.)
Foundation Church (See Spiritualist Camps listing.)

14. *Copper Treatments* (Copper ornaments are available through most jewelry stores, especially those that stock a variety of American Indian jewelry.)

15. *Coué's Autosuggestion*
International Christian Science Center, Boston, Mass. 02115 (800) 225-7090
Norman Vincent Peale Center, Marble Collegiate Church, 1 W. 29th St., New York, N.Y. 10001
Inner Vision, Inc. (See Spiritualist Camps listing.)

17. *Dietetics and Vitamins* (Natural and/or organic vitamins are available through most health food stores.)
American Vegan Society, Malaga, N.J. 08328 (609) 694-2887. (Publishes monthly magazine AHIMSA information on vegetarian diet and seminar.)
People's School of Health, Box 4525, Arcata, Calif. 95521. (Instruction in nutrition, herbology and midwifery.)
Hippocrates Health Institute, 25 Exeter St., Boston, Mass. 02116 (617) 267-4183. (Workshops and classes in nutrition and healing; also see Nature Cure [Clinics].)
Research, Box 5, Pacific Palisades, Calif. 90272. (Publishes *Vegetarian Nutritional Guide*.)
Oriental Medicine Society, 359 Boylston St., Boston, Mass. 02116 (617) 734-3853. (Information on macrobiotic diet and oriental medicine.)
George Ohsawa Macrobiotic Foundation, 1471 10th Ave., San Francisco, Calif. 94122
Institute of Nutritional Research, Box 3413, Los Angeles, Calif. 90028. (Newsletter on current nutritional research.)

Hering Family Health Clinic, 2340 Ward St., Berkeley, Calif.
94705. (Health care, nutrition, acupuncture, homeopathy,
workshops and counseling.)

Trade Associations—These are concerned with retail health
food activities, but if approached properly can supply information.

National Health Federation, Box 688, Monrovia, Calif.
91016. (Newsletter on nutrition and relative activities.)

New Jersey Chapter Natural Food Associates, Inc., c/o Elliot
Pasternack, 361D Crowellis Rd., Highland Park, N.J.
08904. (Information on membership and activities.)

Rocky Mountain Natural Foods Association, 2201 Washington
Blvd., Ogden, Utah 84401. (Concerned with intercommu-
nity relations between all aspects of natural foods commerce.)

National Nutritional Foods Association, c/o Director of Public Information, 7727 S. Painter Ave., Whittier, Calif.
90602. (Major organization concerned with all aspects of
retail and nutritional food activity.)

18. Eye Diagnosis (Iridology)
Dr. Bernard Jensen, c/o Hidden Valley Health Ranch, Route
4, Box 882, Escondido, Calif. 92025 (714) 745-2742.
(Contact for source information only.)

19. Earth Therapy There are many earth products sold in
most health food stores, i.e., Food Therapy Mineral Bath,
etc. Inquire which is best for your needs, or just take your
shoes off and walk on the earth anywhere at any time (of
course with certain obvious considerations).

20. Fasts for Healing (See Nature Cure [Clinics].)

21. Fingernail Diagnosis This falls into the basic category of
hand analysis (See bibliography). Information and readings
(as taught by William G. Benham) may be obtained through:
Ann Koernig, 64 W. 9th St., New York, N.Y. 10011 (212)
533-0323; and Mrs. Florens Meschter, 162 W. 56th St.,
New York, N.Y. 10019. (Neither of these women pro-
fesses to diagnose in her work.)
Metaphysical Center and Book Shop, 420 Sutter Ave., San

Francisco, Calif.   94102 (415) 781-0732. (Classes in palmistry as well as other subjects. H. G. White, Director.)

23. *Foot Zone Therapy* (*Reflexology*) For information and/or treatment contact:

National Institute of Reflexology, Box 948, Rochester, N.Y. 14603. (Eunice Ingham, Accrediting Center.)

Joseph Graziano, 2207 W. Clarendon Ave., Phoenix, Ariz. 85015 (602) 248-8210

Reflexology Center, 1307 Ave. J, Brooklyn, N.Y.   11230 (212) 951-6482

The Sharing Place, 110 W. Mission, Santa Barbara, Calif. 93101. (Classes in reflexology, herbology, meditation, etc.)

Reflex Self-Massager, Dr. Knoll Product, Box 2336, E. Liverpool, Ohio   43920. (Or a rubber ball, golf ball, rolling pin, or similar object may be used to roll with the foot.)

24. *Gravitonics*—American Machine Foundry, Whitely, Maywood, N.J.   07607. (Manufactures an adjustable doorway bar with instructions, for home use.)

25. *Guelphe Fast* (See Dietetics, Herbalism, and/or Nature Cure [Clinics].)

27. *Herbalism* The following are correspondence courses:

Dominion Herbal College, 7527 Kingsway Burnaby 3, B.C., Canada. (Seminars and field trips as well.)

Institute of Herbal Philosophy, Box 968, Glendora, Calif. 91740

School of Natural Healing, Box 352, Provo, Utah   84601

Kwi Tsi Tsa Las Herbal College, Box 46506, Vancouver Postal Station G, B.C. VGR 4G7, Canada. (Seminars.)

Dr. Shooks "Advanced Treatise on Herbology." (This is course material available through a publisher, Health Research, Box 70, Mokelumne Hill, Calif.   95245.)

Christos School of Natural Healing, Box 1503, Taos, N.M. 87571. (Residence classes.)

Membership Organizations—To obtain reliable information on current plant research through journals and seminars, contact:

Economic Botany Society. For membership write: Dr. Harry S.

Fong, c/o College of Pharmacy, University of Illinois Medical Center, Box 6998, Chicago, Ill. 60680. (Generally concerned with the economic use of plants, i.e., for food, industrial use, etc.)

International Institute for Biological and Botanical Research, Box 912, Brooklyn, N.Y. 11202. Specifically relating to the use of plants (herbs) in medicine.

Both are excellent sources for information and are worth becoming members of.

Other sources are:

Natures Botanical Co., 170 Central Ave., Unit 1, Farmingdale, N.Y. 11735. (Complete line of herbal extracts.)

Herb Buyers Guide, Richard Heffern Pyramid Publication, 919 3rd Ave., New York, N.Y. 10022. (An indispensable guide to herbal sources.) $1.25.

United Communications, Box 320, Woodmere, N.Y. 11598. (Unique herbal wall chart as well as a full line of beautifully illustrated color plant-identification charts.)

Herb Trade Association, 3342 Yorba Linda Blvd., Fullerton, Calif. 92631. (Information on local herb suppliers.)

28. Homeopathy
Homeopathic Societies:

American Board of Homeotherapeutics. Vice President, Henry Williams, M.D., 556 W. James St., Lancaster, Pa. 17603.

American Foundation for Homeopathy. President, Wyrth P. Baker, M.D., 4701 Willard Ave., Chevy Chase, Md. 20015.

American Institute of Homeopathy. Secretary, Roy Ruch, D.O., 1541 State St., Schenectady, N.Y. 12304.

The Council for Homeopathic Research and Education, Inc. President, Claude H. Schmidt, Ph.D., Room 812, 36 W. 44th St., New York, N.Y. 10036.

Foundation for Homeopathic Research, Inc. Secretary-Treasurer, John T. Stearn, Ph.D., 3 E. 85th St., New York, N.Y. 10028.

Homeopathic Information Service of the American Institute of Homeopathy, Executive Committee, James Stephenson, M.D., 66 E. 83rd St., New York, N.Y. 10028.

International Homeopathic League. Vice President for America, Frederic Schmid, 6200 Geary St., San Francisco, Calif. 94121.

National Center for Homeopathy. President, Roger Ehrhart, 17 No. Wabash Ave., Chicago, Ill.   60602.

American Board of Homeotherapeutics. Vice President, Henry Williams, M.D., 556 W. James St., Lancaster, Pa.   17603.

Southern Homeopathic Medical Association. Secretary-Treasurer, Benjamin Goldberg, M.D., 22 W. 7th St., Cincinnati, Ohio   45202.

Homeopathic Pharmacies

Boston Medicine Company, 10601 W. Warren, Dearborn, Mich.   48126.

Boericke & Tafel, 1011 Arch Street, Philadelphia, Pa.   19107.

Ehrhart & Karl, Inc., 17 N. Wabash Ave., Chicago, Ill.   60602.

Haussman's Pharmacy, 534–36 Girard Ave., Philadelphia, Pa. 19107.

Humphreys Medicine Company, 63 Meadow Rd., Rutherford, N.J.   07070.

Loytas Pharmaceutical Company, 4200 Laclede Ave., St. Louis, Mo.   63108.

29. Hypnosis for Healing and Diagnosis

The Society for Clinical and Experimental Hypnosis, 205 W. End Ave., New York, N.Y.   10023 (212) 873-7200.

The American Society for Clinical Hypnosis, 240 Devon Ave., Suite 218, Des Plaines, Ill.   60018.

30. Ions for Health

Paul Hampton, Suite 2709, 88 W. Schiller, Chicago, Ill. 60610. (For information only.)

31. Jewels as Therapeutic Agent (See Spiritualist Camps listing.)

32. Kneipp's Water Therapy

Sebastian Kneipp Schule, D. 8939 Bad Worishofen, Postfach 180, West Germany. (Hydrotherapy, School 3 months using the Kneipp system.)

34. Miracle Cures (See Spiritualist Camps listing.)

35. Mucous-free Diet Therapy (See Nature Cure [Clinics].)

222

36. Music as Therapy (See Spiritualist Camps listing.)

Mary Bassano, 275 Lake Oak Place, Bricktown, N.J. 08723. (Color Therapy, teacher and licensed therapist.)

37. Nature Cure (*Clinics:* Dietetics, fasts, exercise, sunbathing, etc.)

Hidden Valley Health Ranch, Rt. 4, Box 822, Escondido, Calif. 92025.

Hippocrates Health Institute, 25 Exeter St., Boston, Mass. 02116.

Herbert Shelton's Nature Cure Clinic, Bulverde, Tex. 78163 (512) 497-3613.

Jacumba Hot Springs Spa, Box 466 L, Jacumba, Calif. 92034

New Age Beauty and Health Farm, 48 Haverstraw Rd., Suffern, N.Y. 10901 (914) 357-7308. (Fasts, Yoga, etc.)

40. Osteopathy

American Osteopathic Association, 212 E. Ohio St., Chicago, Ill. 60611. (National Headquarters.)

Osteopathic Physicians and Surgeons of California, Suite 3, 31582 Coast Highway S., Laguna Beach, Calif. 92651.

Oregon Osteopathic Association, 15745 S.E. Monner, Portland, Ore. 97236.

Michigan Association of Osteopathic Physicians and Surgeons, Inc., 33100 Freedom Rd., Farmington, Mich. 48024.

Florida Osteopathic Association, Suite 1, 161 N. Causeway, New Smyrna Beach, Fla. 32069.

41. Phrenology (Also see Spiritualist Camps listing.)

Ann Koernig, 64 W. 9th St., New York, N.Y. 10011. (Does Phrenology and Scientific Hand Reading.)

43. Physical Culture as Therapy

American Physical Fitness Research Institute, Box 49024, Bel Air, Calif. 90049. (Articles and reports on title subject.)

The Rehabilitation Center, 162 W. 54th St., New York, N.Y. 10019 (212) JU 2-4322. (Workshops, physical therapy, posture, weight control, etc.)

44. Physiotherapy

N.Y.S. Society of Physiotherapists, 7 Edna Dr., Syosset, N.Y. 11791 (516) 921-8585.

Council of Licensed Physiotherapists of N.Y.S., c/o Alan Leventhal, Ph.T., 1818 Newkirk Ave., Brooklyn, N.Y.   11226.
United Society of Physiotherapists, c/o Patrick Trotta, Ph.T., 40–24 Taylor Rd., Fairlawn, N.J.   07410.
American Physical Therapy Association, 1156 15th St. N.W., Washington, D.C.   20005.
Golden State Physical Therapy Association of California, c/o Merlin Kemp, Ph.T., 809 Chapala St., Santa Barbara, Calif.   93101.

45. Priessnitz Water Cures (See Nature Cure [Clinics].)

46. Psychometry (Also see Spiritualist Camps listing.)
Agatha Wehner Wojciechowsky, 334 E. 83rd St., New York, N.Y.   10028 (212) 737-8082. (Classes in psychometry and psychic healing.)

49. Raisin Cure (Most health food stores sell organic raisins.)

50. Reichian Therapeutics
For information contact:
Chester M. Raphael, M.D., 69–17 Fleet St., Forest Hills, N.Y.   11375. (Be specific in your request for information. General information may easily be obtained from large assortment of books on the subject. See Bibliography.)

51. Rikli's Sunshine Cure (See Nature Cure [Clinics].)

52. Saunas (See local listings in yellow pages under Saunas.)

53. Schroth Therapy (See Nature Cure [Clinics].)

54. Sleep Therapy
Inner Vision Inc. (in the Spiritualist Camps listing.) (Class in sleep therapy.)

55. Spiritual Healing (See Spiritualist Camps listing.)

59. Urine Analysis (Most pharmacies sell test paper for urine diagnosis.)

60. Yoga
Ananda Marga Yoga Society, 3453 E. 12th St., Wichita, Kans.   67200 (316) 685-8667.
Dasashram Satsang Centers, Lokoya Tapoyan, Napa, Calif.

94558 (Bhakti, Raja, Karma, Jnana, Tantra, and Laya yoga techniques taught.)

Divine Light Mission, 1560 Race St., Denver, Colo. 80210.

3HO c/o Guru Ram Das Ashram (See Breathing Therapy.)

Integral Yoga Institute (See Breathing Therapy.)

International Babaji Kriya Yoga Sangam, 15712 Longworth Ave., Norwalk, Calif. 90650 (213) 864-6834.

International Sivananda Yoga and Vedanta Society (Hatha and Raja yoga), 5178 St. Lawrence Blvd., Montreal, Quebec, Canada (514) 279-3545.

International Society for Krishna Consciousness, 3764 Watseka Ave., Los Angeles, Calif. 90034 (213) 836-9286.

Radha Soami (Lord of Soul), c/o Roland De Vries, 2922 Las Flores, Arlington (Riverside), Calif. 92503. (Yoga of sound current.) (714) 688-8683.

Ruhani Satsang (Science of the Soul), c/o Kirpal Bhavan, 11404 Lakin Pl., Oakton, Va. 22124 (703) 385-9699.

Self Realization Fellowship, 3880 San Rafael Ave., Los Angeles, Calif. 90065.

Shree Guru Siddha Yoga Ashram (Muktananda) 88 E. 10th St., New York, N.Y. 10000. (Siddha, Raja and Hatha Yoga.)

Sri Chinmoy Center, Inc., 85–45 149th St., Jamaica Hills, Queens, N.Y. 11435 (212) 523-3471.

SAI, 7720 Sunset Blvd., Los Angeles, Calif. 90046 (213) 876-5011 (Sri Satya Sai Baba).

SIMS, 1015 Gayley Ave., Los Angeles, Calif. 90024 (213) 478-1569. (Maharishi Yogi. TM.)

Yoga Institute of Washington, Inc., 1629 K St. N.W., Suite 539A, Washington, D.C. 20006. (All aspects of yoga.)

INDEX

A GUIDE TO ALTERNATIVE MEDICINE

Donald Law, the author of this work, enjoyed a mixed education; Belgian, French, and later German and Danish. Most people finish their studies and graduate by 25, but Donald Law continued learning, and qualifying, until nearly twice that age.

A Doctor of Philosophy, of Botanic Medicine and of Literature, he holds diplomas for psychology, dietetics and other related subjects.

When not traveling in connection with his research studies he climbs, shoots, enjoys sailing etc. He holds several medals for running, life-saving, etc. Paints in oils, plays guitar and chess.

He has been awarded two honorary professorships, one English, the other French. He has translated for major publishing houses.